THE WORLD TEACHER
FOR ALL HUMANITY

BENJAMIN CREME

Share International Foundation
Amsterdam • London

D0954851

*The cover picture is reproduced from a painting
by Benjamin Creme entitled* **Invocation**, *(1964).*

TABLE OF CONTENTS

Benjamin Creme

PREFACE

As Maitreya, the World Teacher, stands poised ready to emerge into full public work, we have brought together in this book an overview of the background to this momentous event. It is based on the keynote talk at the Share International Network Conference near San Francisco, USA, in August 2004, and is largely a commentary on a number of articles written by my Master for our magazine *Share International* between 1987 and 2002, with associated questions from America and Holland; and a compilation from public lectures given in Tokyo and Osaka, Japan, in 2003 and 2006. This is not just simply an aerial 'glance' at the subject but a rather full account of the many ramifications which will flow from this momentous planetary happening.

The book details the planned return of our planetary Hierarchy and the descent of Maitreya from His Himalayan retreat in July 1977 and of His work in the world, albeit behind the scenes, since then. It speaks too of the enormous changes that His presence has brought about; of His plans and projects, and His priorities and recommendations in the immediate future time. It shows Him as a great and powerful Avatar and, at the same time, as a friend and brother of humanity.

Maitreya's advice will bring humanity to a simple choice between two lines of action: to ignore His recommendations and continue in our present mode of life, and so face self-destruction; or to accept gladly His counsel to inaugurate a system of sharing and justice which will guarantee a peaceful and prosperous future for humanity, and the creation of a civilization based on the inner divinity of all men. Maitreya is in no doubt of the choice we will make and looks forward to the open continuation of His mission on our behalf.

Benjamin Creme
London, March 2007

Benjamin Creme lecture, Osaka, Japan, 2006

AN OVERVIEW

The following article is edited from Benjamin Creme's public lectures in Tokyo in 2003 and in Osaka in 2006, and presents an overview of the emergence of the World Teacher and the Masters of Wisdom.

Much of what I have to say is already known, or if not known, easily available. Beginning in 1875, some of this information has already been published in books translated into many languages, and is available to anyone who takes the trouble to read them. The great disciple, Helena Petrovna Blavatsky, founder of the Theosophical Society, began the dissemination of this information. She lived for three years in the Himalayan mountains with the Masters of Whom I shall speak. Her work was followed in 1924 by that of another great Russian disciple, Helena Roerich, through whom the Agni Yoga teachings were given to the world, and by a great English disciple, Alice A. Bailey, between 1919 and 1949.

I have been able to bring these teachings up to date, to show what is actually happening in the process of the return of the Masters to the everyday world. It is from my own personal experiences and contacts that I make these assertions. But I am not asking you to believe me. I am simply presenting my information to you for your consideration. If it appears to you to be reasonable and rational, if it seems to relate to present events, the happenings of the world that are taking place and have been for many years, if in a word it has for you the ring of truth, then by all means believe it, but otherwise not. I am perfectly conscious that much of this information will appear strange and perhaps unbelievable to some of you. If that is the case, please be assured that I shall not be the slightest bit offended or even disappointed. But if this information at least allows you to hope for a better future for yourself and your children, I shall be perfectly satisfied.

Tension and Crisis

What the world needs now is the removal of fear and the renewal of hope. We are going through one of the greatest periods of tension since the end of the Cold War. This particular phase of tension and crisis began on 11 September 2001.

On that day, an attack by foreign terrorists took place on the World Trade Center in New York and the Pentagon in Washington, DC, as well as a foiled attack on the White House. It was an attack not only on America, but on American power, represented by the Pentagon and the White House, and the major industrial nations of the world through the attack on the World Trade Center. That terrible, dramatic attack took America and the entire world by surprise and shock. The world has been in a state of shock ever since. But I suggest it should not have taken the world so much by surprise. It was one of the most daring, most audacious and most organized of many such attacks on the Western world.

That attack resulted in an attack on Afghanistan in which more ordinary, innocent citizens of Afghanistan were killed than were killed in the World Trade Center on 11 September. This was followed by the American and British attack on Iraq, and the continuing occupation in which hundreds of thousands of innocent Iraqi citizens have also lost their lives.

The American, British and other governments have not recognized that the attack on the World Trade Center and Pentagon, and the foiled attack on the White House, have a cause. It is the effect of a cause. In other words, it is karmic. It is the result of the Law of Karma, the Law of Cause and Effect.

The cause is complex, but put very simply, it is the extreme difference in living standards between the developed Western world and the developing world. One-third of the world — mainly America, Europe, Japan, Australia, and Canada — usurp and greedily waste three-quarters of the world's food, and some 83 per cent of all other resources. The developing world, the so-called Third World, has to make due with the rest, distributed among two-thirds of the world's population.

This division is the result of greed, lack of compassion, and complacency. It is unfair and extraordinarily dangerous for the security of the world. The developing world will not for ever put up with this state of affairs. They will demand their fair share of the world's resources. The first steps in that direction were the attacks on America. The greatest danger to the world was not the existence of Iraq, with its dictatorship, nor is it Iran with its fundamentalist Muslim attitudes and lack of respect for America, or North Korea with its military potential. The greatest danger is the discrepancy in living standards between the developed and the developing world.

Humanity is taking a long time to understand these problems, the true problems that beset it today. But unless it understands these problems, there will be no hope for the future of the world. The tensions existing in this discrepancy of living standards have within them the seeds of a third world war. That war would be nuclear and would destroy all life on the planet.

I am a very optimistic person by nature. I tend to look on the brighter side of life, and am not too depressed by gloomy thoughts of the world's destruction. But if I did not know what I do know, I would have little hope that humanity would survive, little hope that in time humanity would awaken to the real problems that beset it, and begin to change. I am very doubtful that on our own we would do that.

Fortunately, I do not believe that we are alone, without help, without guidance. There has stood behind humanity, from the earliest days of its existence, a group of men of extraordinary insight and wisdom, called the Masters of Wisdom, the Spiritual Hierarchy of our planet.

The Masters of the Spiritual Hierarchy

This group of men have gone ahead of us in evolution. They have come to a point where They need no further incarnational experience on Earth, but nevertheless remain to act as a kind of inner government of the world. The Masters are the Custodians of the Plan of evolution that is driving humanity forward and upward, whether we are aware of it or not. They have brought humanity from the stage of early animal man and woman to the point where we are today — guiding, protecting and stimulating the evolutionary advance of all people.

Sometimes They have worked more openly, but for the last 98,000 years, with very few exceptions, They have lived in the remote mountain and desert areas of the world, such as the Himalaya, the Andes, the Rockies, the Carpathians, the Urals, and the Gobi Desert and other deserts. From these mountain and desert areas, working mainly through Their disciples, men and women in the world, They have guided humanity along the evolutionary path with Their love and wisdom.

For over 500 years the Masters have known that sooner or later They would be required to come back into the everyday world, known to us for what They are. This pertains to Their own evolution, quite separate from the human evolution. The only question was when humanity would be ready for the return to the everyday world of such spiritual giants. Until relatively recently, it was thought it would probably be 1,200 or 1,300 years yet before we would be ready to receive men of that kind of spiritual potency into our everyday world.

But in June 1945, at the end of the Second World War, Maitreya, the head and leader of that group of perfected men, announced His decision to return at the earliest possible moment into the world, along with a large number of His group. Maitreya said that He would come when a measure of peace had been established in the world, when the energy we call goodwill, which the Masters see as the lowest aspect of love, was manifesting and leading to the establishment of correct human relationships, and when the religious and political groups were putting their houses in order. These conditions did not have to be perfectly met, but when our minds were at least moving in these directions, Maitreya said that He would come without fail at the earliest possible moment.

The coming of Maitreya was foretold 2,600 years ago by Gautama Buddha, Who said that at this time would come another great teacher, a Buddha like Himself by the name Maitreya Who, by dint of His colossal spiritual stature, would galvanize and inspire humanity to create a brilliant golden civilization based, as He put it, on righteousness and truth.

Every manifestation of a Teacher that has occurred from the earliest times has been a disciple overshadowed by the Teacher. Historically they are known as Hercules, Hermes, Rama, Mithra, Vyasa, Confucius, Zoroaster, Krishna, Shankaracharya, Gautama, Jesus and Mohammed. These have all been disciples overshadowed by the teacher Himself. Just as the Buddha worked through the Prince Gautama, so in Palestine Maitreya worked through Jesus of Nazareth.

Maitreya is the embodiment of what we call the Christ Principle, the energy of Love. Maitreya is so advanced, so pure, He can embody in His own being, and not simply channel, the energy of Love, the second aspect of God. Through Jesus He showed that Love of God in its perfection in a man for the first time, just as through the Prince Gautama, the Buddha showed the Wisdom aspect of God in its perfection in a man for the first time.

Now, for the first time in history, the Teacher has come into the world Himself. Maitreya is the head and leader of His group of disciples, the Masters of Wisdom, and holds the office of World Teacher. He has held this office for the last 2,000

7

years, appearing through Jesus, and will be the World Teacher for this coming age, the age of Aquarius, which is now beginning and will last about 2,350 to 2,500 years.

For thousands of years, Maitreya has lived in retreat in the high Himalaya. But Maitreya arrived in the everyday world — He has never been away from the world — on 19 July 1977. On 8 July, Maitreya descended from His mountain retreat in a self-made body, constructed especially for this mission in the world. This body allows Him to live at our level of existence, and at the same time be sensitive enough to bring in His consciousness as the World Teacher. Maitreya stayed on the plains in Pakistan for some days to acclimatize that body, and on 19 July came by plane into London, England. He has made the Asian community of London what He calls His point of focus in the modern world.

Beginning of a New Age

What do I mean by the coming age of Aquarius? Let me illustrate it in astronomical terms, because it is an astronomical fact that we are entering a New Age. The solar system of which we are a part makes a journey in space that takes, relative to the constellations, about 25,000-26,000 years to complete. Therefore every approximately 2,150 years our sun comes into a particular alignment, an energetic relationship, with each of the constellations in turn. When the sun is in that alignment, we say we are in the age of that particular constellation.

For the last 2,150 years that alignment was with the constellation Pisces. We have been in the age of Pisces, and that age has come to an end. The sun has moved away from the sphere of influence of the energies of Pisces and is entering the same relationship with the constellation Aquarius, and therefore, with the energies of Aquarius. The energies of Pisces began to be withdrawn in 1625. The energies of Aquarius began to come in and affect our planet in 1675. Today there is a kind of balance.

The energies of Pisces and the energies of Aquarius are, as far as we are concerned, more or less equal, and that is our problem. The energies of Pisces are being withdrawn and have left all the structures that were built under their influence: political, economic, religious, social, scientific, educational, cultural and so on. All these structures have become crystallized. They are extant, but they no longer have the energy that brought them into being, so they do not work any more. As we have responded to the energies of Pisces, they have completely split the world into tiny fragmented parts.

The energies of Aquarius, which are mounting in potency with every day that passes, work on us in a very different way. They have a completely different effect on humanity. They are the energies of synthesis. As the energies of Pisces have divided the world, the energies of Aquarius will draw humanity together, blending and fusing humanity into one group.

At the start of every new age, from the beginning of time, a Teacher from the Spiritual Hierarchy of Masters has come into the world to inaugurate the age, set in motion the ideas that would uplift and galvanize humanity, bringing it forward in its evolution, and creating conditions in which this could be done.

Establishment of Peace

Maitreya's plans are to awaken humanity to the perils before it and show humanity how to avoid self-destruction. Maitreya says it is really very simple for humanity if we could take the first step.

Humanity needs above all to establish peace. Without peace there will be no future for humanity because we have the nuclear capacity to destroy the world and all life, human and subhuman alike. How do we get peace? That is the es-

9

sential question. Certainly not using the methods of the American and British governments in recent times when they attack one country after another. That is certainly not going to give peace to the world. It will not even end terrorism in the world. There will never be an end to terrorism until the world itself has changed.

Only one thing will create peace and the end of terrorism — the creation of a just world. If there is no justice, there will never be peace. If there is no justice, there is no hope for any of us because everybody in the world will die unless we establish justice in the world. There is only one way to establish justice and that is to share the resources of the world more equitably. It is so simple and yet we refrain from doing it. Without sharing there will never be justice. Without justice there will never be peace. Without peace there is no future for us.

So what do we have to do? The developed nations have to realize that the world's food and resources belong to everyone, are given by divine providence for all the peoples of the world, not just the developed nations who have the money to buy the food and resources. They have the money to buy because they are more advanced technologically, more advanced in industry perhaps. But the goods they produce do not give value to the resources and activities of the people of the Third World. This approach is cavalier, dishonest, greedy and selfish, and has to change, otherwise there is no future for the world.

The Masters of the Spiritual Hierarchy have plans for the redistribution of the world's resources, which will be presented as soon as humanity says: "You are right. We believe that the only way is by sharing better the resources. How do we do it?"

It is simple to do. Probably the most simple thing to do is that first step into sharing. People imagine things in a purely personal way. They say: "Oh, my goodness. Sharing? Are they going to take my money out of the bank and send it to Indonesia or Africa to people that I do not know?" It is actually very different from that. It will be done at national and international levels.

Each nation will be asked to make an inventory of what it has and what it needs, what it produces and what it imports. Then each nation will be asked to make over in trust for the world as a whole into a common pool that which it has in excess of its needs. Out of that common pool the needs of all can be met. Will that end terrorism in the world? Probably not at first. But it is the first step into the creation of justice in the world, and will create the essential for that correct relation that we call trust.

When we create trust we can do marvels. We can do what is impossible without it. When countries trust each other, they can talk to each other without fear. With the creation of trust through sharing of resources, we can begin to solve all the world's problems one after the other. They become approachable and easily solvable and the world can be changed very quickly indeed.

And with that creation of trust through sharing, we can overcome the situation of today of people who are filled with anger and resentment. They are filled with the sense of injustice, and they see no way for their children to be given a decent life, and so they turn, some of them, to terrorism.

Maitreya's Teachings

Maitreya's teachings demonstrate and affirm the interconnectedness of everything in the world. This is the rationale of the Law of Karma, the Law of Cause and Effect. Recently in the United States there was an earthquake measuring 4.9 in the east, in an area that is not normally prone to earthquakes. Through the midwestern United States, Kansas and the central states, there have been hundreds of tornadoes one after the

11

other for days, leaving paths of destruction 400 miles wide and killing many people.

These are called acts of nature, acts of God. But they are in this case a result of the Law of Karma. The crisis that manifested itself as the SARS infection in China and elsewhere, for example, the epidemics of flu throughout Europe, are the direct results of the fear generated from the crisis conditions set up by the US attacks on Afghanistan and Iraq. It is not a question of God punishing the aggressor. It is a simple law of the interconnectedness of all atoms in the universe. What happens here sets up something that will inevitably happen elsewhere by the law of action and reaction.

When humanity truly understands this law, the Law of Karma, not just as an intellectual idea, it will see that every thought, every action, sets into motion a cause or causes. The effects stemming from these causes make our lives for good or ill.

The need for harmlessness in every action in our lives becomes apparent. When we act, we have to know what the result of this action could be. If the action is destructive, it produces destruction in the world. If the action is not destructive, if it is creative, if it is harmless, it creates harmlessness, it creates good in the world.

We have our evolution in our own hands. We are responsible. Every act, every thought is part of the thoughts and actions of all humanity, and affect all humanity. We cannot imagine how far our thought proceeds before it returns as the reaction to a cause. When humanity's thoughts and actions are destructive, when we create thoughtforms of destruction, attack, killing and fear, we generate thereby thoughtforms that impinge on the forces of nature. These forces are under the control of the devic or angelic evolutions. They go out of equilibrium as we are out of equilibrium, and earthquakes, tornadoes, floods, typhoons are the results.

We have to begin to think in a more integrated way, seeing the connection between events, not putting everything into separate categories so they do not relate any more. Everything is related to everything else. Everything impinges on everything else. We have to acquire the insight and intelligent response to our feelings and intuitions about how to live. If we listen to our intuition, if we listen to the heart, we can learn to live in a way that is harmless, that does not cause this greedy, selfish, antagonistic pull between ourselves and society, between our country and another country.

Everybody in the world without exception is looking for, aiming towards, longing for, the experience of unity. Equilibrium reflects the underlying unity of all people. But our modern world is built on competition, the opposite of equilibrium. You have to win, you have to do something better, cheaper, quicker, more aggressively, than somebody else. Everybody is locked into competition, and they do not give their intuition the room to breathe, to live, to give them the sense of their own longing for unity. We are locked into competition and what we need is co-operation. Co-operation reflects the longing for unity, the longing for equilibrium, which is the only possible, creative way to proceed in evolution.

Co-operation takes awareness. We have to be aware of what is happening to us. If we are not aware, we become like a machine, antagonistic and destructive, the opposite of what we need and what we are, which is a co-operative, creative person who longs to create co-operatively with others and demonstrate the unity of the world. Everyone without exception at some level has that ideal because we are all part of the one humanity.

Maitreya's Emergence

Maitreya as World Teacher is awaiting an opportunity to present His teachings directly to humanity. Between 1988 and

1991 Maitreya gave a series of predictions about world events, which were given to us to publish in our magazine *Share International.*(*) One of the first of these predictions was that there will be a world stock-exchange crash that will begin in Japan. That seemed an extraordinary statement at the time. In mid-1988 the Nikkei average stood at 40,000 points. In 1990 it began to fall. And the Japanese who know these things said that if it comes to 18,000 points, that is the end. It came down to 10,000 points and then 7,000 points. As a result, like dominoes followed all the countries of the Pacific Rim — Malaysia, Indonesia, Hong Kong and Singapore. They all began to crash as a result of the Japanese crash. And then Russia, Brazil and Argentina.

The United States and European stock markets have been going up and down, up and down, but do not actually follow through as they have done in Japan. Maitreya is waiting for the collapse of the US and European economies to come forward, to present Himself to the world, to start His public teaching. But events in the world are so critical, with so much tension and fear, that Maitreya is concerned to come forward as soon as possible. He is taking every opportunity to present Himself closer and closer to the groups who are working for the Reappearance but also on a wider scale to the people in the world.

He talks to people at all levels, ordinary people and those most useful at every level — political, economic, social, scientific, educational, and so on — people who can help the world, who have influence for good in the world. In this way He has built up a great body of people who in the immediate future will begin the changes necessary to transform the world for the better.

When Maitreya comes forward, He will not at first use the name Maitreya. He will present Himself as an ordinary person, although, of course, an extraordinary person. He will appear at first in America on television on a large network, and then in Japan and around the world. He will become known for His analysis of the world's needs. Look for a man who is calling for justice for all the world, freedom for all the world.

When enough people are responding to what He has to say, Maitreya will be asked to speak to the entire world. On that day, the Day of Declaration, as it will be known, you will see a now-familiar face on television, that of Maitreya. The television networks of the world will be linked together by satellite, which are actually in place for this event. And then an extraordinary thing will happen. Simultaneously throughout the world people will see Maitreya's face on their television sets. Maitreya is omniscient and omnipresent, and everyone above the age of 14 will hear His words, His thoughts, His ideas inwardly, silently, telepathically in their own language. As you are watching this face, His lips will not move, He will not speak, but His ideas will come into your mind. The French will hear Him in French, the Germans in German, the English in English, the Dutch in Dutch, the Japanese in Japanese, and so on throughout the world. Whatever you are doing, if you are out fishing or under the car, if you are not watching television, you will still hear the voice, the thoughts, the ideas of Maitreya inwardly. This miracle is a repetition, only now on a world scale, of the true happenings of Pentecost 2,000 years ago. Also in this way Maitreya will foreshadow the future ability of all people to communicate mentally, telepathically at will over any distance.

Maitreya will give a short history of the long history of the world, and show the height from which humanity has fallen into the materialism of today. He will introduce the fact of His group, the Spiritual Hierarchy of Masters. He will show the future, and outline some of the extraordinary scientific marvels that will open up new life for humanity. He will make His appeal for justice, for sharing as the only way to justice, and so to peace in the world.

While this is taking place His energy, the energy of Love, will flow out in tremendous potency through the hearts of all. This will invoke an intuitive, heartfelt response to the message. He has said: "It will be as if I embrace the whole world. People will feel it even physically." On the dense-physical plane there will be hundreds of thousands of spontaneous miracle healings, cures throughout the world.

In these three ways you will know that that Man and, of course, only that Man, is the World Teacher awaited by the Christians as the Christ, by Muslims as the Imam Mahdi, by Jews as the Messiah, by Hindus as Krishna or Kalki Avatar, by Buddhists under His name, Maitreya Buddha, by people of no religious affiliation who simply wish for a better life for all.

Our response to this event will determine the entire future of the world. Maitreya will present to us a choice; we have free will and the choice is ours. Simply put, it is a choice for sharing, justice and the end of war and terrorism for ever, or the eventual annihilation of all life on Earth, human and sub-human alike. Maitreya has already said: "My heart tells me your answer, your choice, and is glad."

(*) These series of Maitreya's forecasts and teachings have been compiled and published in the book *Maitreya's Teachings — the Laws of Life.*

THE WORLD TEACHER
FOR ALL HUMANITY

The following article is an edited version of a talk given by Benjamin Creme at the Transmission Meditation Conference held near San Francisco, USA, in August 2004.

THE EMERGENCE OF MAITREYA

"For several years, many people have awaited, with varying degrees of patience, the emergence of Maitreya into the arena of the world, to present Himself to the people as the World Teacher for Aquarius. Many have found it a tiresome wait indeed, while others have cheerfully worked to acquaint the world of His presence and plans, knowing that eventually their efforts would succeed. The day has dawned when all will see Him. Knowingly or not, all have called Him and He has kept His promise to return." *('The emergence of Maitreya', by the Master —, SI, April 1987)**

"Many have found it a tiresome wait indeed." If you knew Maitreya better than you in fact do, you would know that He believes that He *has* returned. He really believes that all this talk of when is He going to come out is a nonsense. He has already done it. When He visits groups — of course, not dressed or looking like Maitreya (but in various disguises) — they know Who He is because He has been confirmed by my Master to have been Maitreya. Then He comes again looking just like the same gentleman and they ask Him questions and He replies — and then they say: "But oh, it takes so long! What gets me is the state of the world, and it is so long a wait. How do I explain to people that it has to take time?" He says: "What are you talking about? You can be as anxious as you like, but it is foolish. There is nothing to be anxious about." "The world is fine, full of promise. Maitreya is here. He has returned. You do not have anything to wait for; it is done — the plan is working well."

The world is in a state of change which we cannot even begin to see, so involved are we, naturally, in the events of the last few years: since 9/11, for instance, followed by the attack on Afghanistan, and the invasion of Iraq that is still going on — not to mention the possibilities of greater terror.

The decade before 9/11 was one of growing calm, growing change for the better. Extraordinary things happened: the end of the Cold War, for example, an extraordinary happening, the greatest event in the world since the end of World War II. It lifted from humanity the fear of sudden death — not just the possibility of it, almost the likelihood of a catastrophic end of everything. People stopped having children because they did not want to bring them into a world which was going to be destroyed. Now people have children, they look forward to it, and they know that their children are going to live and build a new civilization.

People experienced in the 10 to 12 years before 9/11 an extraordinary transformation of the world. For the people involved, some of these were tremendous, climactic: the changes that occurred in the Soviet Union, the collapse of the political system, the demands of millions of people for a better and easier lifestyle, and the rise into prominence of the now mega-rich oilmen of Russia; the Chinese experiment which has steadily brought a large section of the population into a material abundance which they have never known before. None of the people in China had experienced the quality of life or the material affluence that the eastern seaboard of China now does. Perhaps 20 million people can now experience the material well-being of the more affluent parts of Europe and America. This is altogether new and has alleviated elsewhere

18

in China a tremendous amount of poverty. It is true that there are sections of China which are still poor, but as a whole China has come out of the agonizing poverty which it knew before. Likewise, most of the Russian people are finding life easier, if emptier.

People in the West — America, Europe — have found a growing interdependence, a recognition of the oneness of humanity and the necessity of seeing the world as one, and that real changes are possible only on a global scale.

One of the major events of the last few years, and for the first time in history, was that millions of people were allowed to be full and equal citizens and recognized owners of their own country. It was an extraordinary happening, the release of Nelson Mandela and the creation of the new South Africa. That was the direct work of Maitreya; He brought it about.

Likewise, His influence opened up the Soviet Union to *glasnost*, welcoming the Soviet Union into the community of nations, and hence the transformation of the old, angry *nyet*-sounding bear into a friendly, co-operative federation of nations. It is a tremendous transformation.

There was also the unification of Germany, years ahead of anyone's estimation of the possibility. Some, of course, those of the West, see it as a new responsibility which has lowered their standard of living (which was artificially high), but it has given a new stability to Europe which, as you know, was in a constantly warring state right up to the 1940s.

So, a tremendous amount has been done, greatly influenced by Maitreya, which we tend to forget. In our anguish, concern for the future and lack of a sense of proportion, we tend to forget the great positive changes which have come about, mainly because of the powerful energies now pouring into the world, and the presence of a large group of extraordinary men, about 14 Masters, and the Master of all the Masters, Maitreya Himself.

"For years He, too, has awaited the invitation from men to emerge and speak for all. Now that, at last, this has been given, He has taken steps to ensure His recognition and acceptance. Not for nothing has He prepared many groups to acknowledge Him. Highly placed and influential, there are those in varied walks of life who know Him to be here, know His plans and priorities, have listened to His words and believe them to be true. From diverse backgrounds and many countries do these prepared ones come, alike in their desire to serve Maitreya and the world. With their detailed knowledge of His plans they will speak for Him, awakening their colleagues and citizens to the task ahead. In this fashion will He work through them, pointing the way to a better future." *('The emergence of Maitreya')*

Despite His readiness for spontaneous action, everything that Maitreya does, as with all the Masters, is done with meticulous care. They spend years and tremendous amounts of directed energy to make sure that a plan works out by appearing to people all over the world: unimportant people, people who expect Him, who would recognize Him if they saw Him at lectures, and so on. It is not always easy to recognize Him because He appears in many different ways: as a woman, a man, an old woman with one tooth, perhaps appearing in beautiful clothes but wearing galoshes or carpet slippers, a little bit odd. That is the hint that is often given. I remember an account of a Master Who appeared dressed superbly in late 19th century clothes — long coat, cravat, and a top hat with a pile of wool and stuff coming out of the top.

Maitreya has created a huge body of men and women who have met Him, with whom He has spent time, outlined His priorities, and talked about the needs of the world; people in all walks of life, royalty, people of power and prestige, heads of government, the diplomatic corps all over the world, people who have influence with government, special envoys, and so on; religious leaders, household names in industry and heads of corporations. There is now a huge group of people who are absolutely familiar with the thoughts, ideas and plans of Maitreya. When He becomes more open, when people actually see Him (although He will not be announced as Maitreya), these people will emerge and talk and agree that it is true: the great Teacher, a World Teacher, is here. They may not point to Him but will say: "He is here. I know. This is His idea."

These people have among them individuals of great following, so that when they speak they will be believed by the masses who just follow a leader; for them they are leaders, of thought, of fashionable ideas, who write for newspapers and magazines, high level media people who have met Maitreya, who know His ideas, His thoughts, His analysis of the requirements for change and for peace. In this way He is building up a huge body of opinion on His side.

Then it will be the time for the masses of people to form a huge, broad, world public opinion which will sweep across the world and force governments to begin the process of change, to implement the teachings of Maitreya.

Some will see Him as the Christ. Some will see Him as perhaps a political/economic thinker who will inspire them and show that there is a possibility for change, that we do not have to follow Mr Bush or Mr Blair and go the old way; that the old methods of divide and rule are over, the old methods of governments who make policies and force them on their peoples are finished. Governments will come to realize, by dint of the manifested power of the people, that their job, their task, is to look after the needs of the people. This will happen in all countries because that is the role of government. Some governments do it to a tiny degree; others do it more. Some governments are more democratic, and there is more participation in the process, but some are extremely dictatorial and the people have little say. This will end.

"Shortly, His face will be seen by thousands around the world. Television has made it possible for the Avatar to enter the homes of countless people and with simple words to penetrate their hearts." *('The emergence of Maitreya')*

One of the secrets of the power of Maitreya, which only a limited number of people have experienced so far (although that is a very large number, it is still limited compared with the population of the world), is the simplicity of His utterance. He speaks straight from the heart to the heart of the person. He is not trying to be clever. He is not trying to argue a case.

He is alerting people to the obvious, but it does not seem to be obvious to many of the governments in the world, although it is obvious to everyone that they need food, shelter, healthcare, education, stimulus, culture and variety in their lives. Everybody knows that, but governments do not on the whole provide these essential needs.

It is the responsibility of governments to do that, and when Maitreya speaks He utters these simple things that most Christians would not expect to hear from the Christ. They expect to hear talks about religion, about God or about one religion as against another, academic religion, religion in the way religionists talk about it or fight about it or worry about it.

He does not come as a religious teacher although He is awaited by all the religious groups under one name or another. And, of course, for the various religious groups it will be an extraordinary surprise, and with great difficulty for many people will He be recognized and followed.

"Soon will follow other such appearances until the whole world listens and responds." *('The emergence of Maitreya')*

He has planned a whole series of appearances. The emergence of Maitreya is taking place literally, as we know, over years and in phases, each phase allowing more and more people to hear Him. He spent years going around the world appearing to people where He has created wells of healing water, charging the wells with cosmic energy from Aquarius. Eventually, I have been told, there will be 777 such sources of water.

He appeared to mainly religious groups and nearly every time a well or source of water was created. If you multiply the audiences by His 239 appearances (1988-2002)** it adds up to a tremendous number of people who have heard Him speak, heard His concerns and His solutions to our problems.

"In this manner, the world will come to know that the Christ, Maitreya, is in our midst, ready to teach and lead, to serve and guide, to show the way back from the abyss and to inspire the creation of a new era for men." ('The emergence of Maitreya')

The Master again and again has used this phrase "to show the way back from the abyss". From the Masters' point of view the world is already saved, but humanity does not know this and has to act upon its best intentions and highest interest, and so draw away from the abyss, the precipice. The abyss, of course, would be war on a world scale. That would be nuclear and would destroy all life on Earth; the human experiment on Earth would cease.

The Masters are sure that Their work, Their gift to humanity of protection and teaching and guidance, will allow humanity, in time, to pull away from the abyss, to change direction. That is the last phase of the work of Maitreya.

When He is working openly in the world, even if not under the name of Maitreya, it will be to bring humanity to that point. When that is reached, when the people are themselves changing direction, He can reveal His true stature and purpose. The Masters see the present situation in Iraq, in America in general with the present administration, as a kind of hiccup in the process of change. They do not see it as a final end that will cause us to go over the abyss.

So for the Masters this is not the 'end game'. The end game is in the minds of fundamentalists who think that there are 'end times', that we are near the end times and that maybe they are contributing. The US President is a fundamentalist Christian who believes God is directing him. I believe he is living in illusion, and I share that belief with millions of others in the USA and abroad. But the effect of it is that many people are, in their minds, and to some extent in their hearts, conditioned by the teachings of the fundamentalists to see these times as the 'Divine Times', the times foretold in their scriptures, and that they are right in line with the 'pronouncements of God' through the Christian scriptures. They are nothing of the kind, but that is what they believe, and they are millions strong.

Many years ago I remember it was claimed that there were 40 million fundamentalist Christians in this country [USA] out of a population of 275 million people; a huge proportion. The fundamentalists are very strong among the religious groups here, whether they be Baptist or Roman Catholics. They each have their branch of fundamentalism and they add up to a huge proportion of the Christians in America.

Maitreya says: "Keep your eye on the prize and the prize is humanity." Maitreya appeared on a march in London in February 2003, and was interviewed for video by a small group of students. Some of our group were nearby. He appeared in the guise of a Caribbean man and He was wonderful. He said: "I am so glad. I am so glad to see all you young people marching for the truth, for peace, and for justice, it is so wonderful to see this." And then He said: "Keep your eyes on the prize, and the prize is humanity!" Then a young man came up to Him, and they 'touched hands'. That younger man was a disciple of one of the Masters. They went off together. So: "Keep your eyes on the prize and the prize is humanity!" ***

"That not all men, at first, will recognize Him, perhaps,

needs to be said. Not all know the true background to His life and advent. But, more and more, they will see the wisdom of His words, feel the blessing of His presence, and know from within their hearts the truth that He utters.

"From within their hearts, too, will they respond, acknowledging Him as the Teacher for the Age. From them will He evoke the desire to share, to recreate a balanced and harmonious world. When men realize the urgency of the task, they will unleash upon the iniquities of the present a force for good unlike aught seen before. The transformation of the world will proceed apace and men will work together as brothers for the good of all. Thus will it be. Thus will the New Age be built by man himself under the guidance of Maitreya and His Group. The separation of the past will give place to co-operation and sharing; the selfishness and greed to a new sense of justice. From within man himself will come the urge for betterment, a testimony to the divinity inherent in us all. That divinity will Maitreya show to be the nature of man, and He the Agent of its manifestation.

"Already, the signs of His work are apparent to all. The old dogmas die; new brooms are sweeping away the debris of the past. The old men linger but a new force of truth beats on their embattled and crumbling walls. Not for long will they with-stand this new force for righteousness and justice." *('The emergence of Maitreya')*

That is how the Masters see the effect of Maitreya when He starts to speak openly in the world. Not all will recognize Him. Some will call Him the Antichrist. They call me the forerun-ner of the Antichrist, the Antichrist's 'leg-man'. I have been called that for a long time.

THE VOICE OF MAITREYA

"With each day that passes, the appearance before the world of the Great Lord grows ever closer. Very soon, now, humanity will know that there lives among them a man of most unusual attributes: a capacity for service conditioned only by the Karmic Law; a knowledge of that law unique even among His peers; a wisdom fashioned from the experience of millennia; from the depth of that experience, a vision of the Purpose embodied in the Plan of God ..." *(The Master —, from 'The voice of Maitreya', SI, July 1994)*

That is the kind of man we are going to see. An extraordinary man, unlike anyone we have ever known before. No one in the world, except perhaps another Master, can speak with the knowledge, the wisdom, the ages-long experience, that Maitreya has. You have to be a Master and you have to know not only the world and all its problems, all it difficulties, all that is needed in the way of change, but also the world of meaning. You have to know the meaning and the purpose of life on Earth. You have to be able to give at least an inkling of that to the humanity of the time. It is one thing being the Christ or being a Master and speaking to humanity, but unless it is in terms that humanity can recognize then nothing would be communicated. So it is an understanding of the problems, and the solutions to the problems, presented to humanity in a way that makes them real, makes them touchable, that we recognize as our own problems and that the way out is a logical and believable answer to them.

That, perhaps, is one of the reasons why more people do not just accept this information, which we might expect they should, because I think probably we do not know how to present it in a way that is totally believable, totally understandable, and is seen as part of their own experience.

If we were a Master, especially Maitreya, we could project into their minds answers, experiences and visions which consolidate the information, make it real for them. That is something which is rare; something which we on the whole cannot do.

That is not to say that we should not try, should not spend as much time and energy as we can on telling the story, making known the fact of the Christ's presence and the nature of His priorities, the need for change and the kinds of change which He sees must take place.

We have to present it in a way that makes it real for people; they have to experience it. You have to make them feel that people are starving to death. Not just words, but they have to experience what starving to death means to some extent. You have to put it into a framework which they will take closer to them and look at, however horrific it might be. To give a list of statistics would go over their heads. Statistics are difficult to take in. You can say 20 per cent of people in the world use 80 per cent of the resources of the world, and it does not mean very much. It is a fact, a terrible fact, but it is easily glossed over. But people can have a vision of the poor, the starving, when they see Maitreya and they hear His concern for the starving millions, because those are the people that He is talking about. He is not talking about the well-fed middle classes in Europe, America and Japan. He is talking and concerned about the millions of people living on a dollar a day or less; the people who have nothing at all, who are all skin and bone and dying in the millions. That is the quality that Maitreya can convey to people with the minimum of excess and with the energy which brings their love and compassion to bear on the problem. And so the response to Maitreya will be altogether different from what *we* could achieve saying the same things. But we should not think that it will be easy.

" . . . an ability to speak, simply, to the hearts of men; an awareness of the needs of men and of how these needs can be assured; a concern and a love for all, boundless, fathomless, beyond all possibility of man's imagining. A Hero, a Titan, is in men's midst, and soon will they awaken to His presence.

"Soon, very soon, now, Maitreya plans to address a large

section of mankind and to acquaint them with His hopes and plans, to share with them His vision of a better world for all. From that time forth, the process of His emergence will continue apace, and, gathering momentum, will bring Him openly before the world. Thus will the Son of Man fulfil His promise to return, and thus will men know that the time of their deliverance is at hand.

"While awaiting an invitation to emerge and speak directly to men, Maitreya has not, you may be sure, stood idly by. Powerful and deep are the transformations which His presence has already wrought, and, even as these words are written and read, further profound changes can be expected to appear.

"A new voice is being heard in the affairs of men, articulated by a few sensitive minds among the leaders of the nations. More and more, this voice will give expression to the foremost needs of our time: peace, tolerance, forgiveness of past wrongs, co-operation and sharing for the benefit of all. That voice will issue from the hearts and minds of all who love their fellow-men, creating an invincible demand for world reconstruction and renewal. That voice is the voice of the new era. It is the voice of Maitreya.

"Add your voice to that gathering clamour for peace and justice and become aware of your place in history. A new world is in the making and requires the involvement of all: all have a part to play in this great undertaking; none should feel too young or too old to voice aloud their aspirations." ('The voice of Maitreya')

Already there are individuals, and soon groups of individuals, who will voice aloud, are already voicing aloud, the needs of the world. We are not alone in expressing the need for justice in order to ensure peace in the world. Many thousands and maybe millions of people believe that to be the case. We are the recipients of knowledge about the presence of Maitreya, and this creates a different situation. But we have to understand and remember that millions of people have inwardly responded to Maitreya, that there are different groups, different kinds of people, people in the political groups and in business and welfare, in the NGOs, who are concerned with the need to transform the distribution system of the world so that people everywhere can live decent lives.

We tend to think, because our task is to make it known that Maitreya is in the world and that the Masters are returning to the world, that it ends there, that we are the only ones with these ideas. But this is not the case. When we understand that these same ideas, if not the Reappearance of the Christ but the same political and economic ideas, are shared by millions of people throughout the world, then you can see it makes our work that much easier. They will not necessarily agree that the Christ is in the world, but that is not important if they agree that the world needs to share, the world needs justice if we are to have peace. That is the important thing.

If only Mr Bush and Mr Blair knew that that truth is behind the events of the coming time, it would change the whole climate for the world. Unfortunately they do not. They only believe in war, at least Mr Bush only believes in war — war as a war on terrorism. It is becoming very popular, 'the war on terrorism', and the war in Iraq, of course, is seen as a war on terrorism, which it is not. That is a lie. These lies are coming out fast, one after the other, and the people of this country [USA] and the world generally, if they did not know the lies before, they certainly know them now.

The time for these little men is ending, these men of little conscience, with not even the respect for their people to say they were wrong, they made mistakes, and to apologize. If they did that, there would be a transformation in their position in each country, and they would perhaps take more account of the minds of their people. But they cannot. They are too arrogant to do that.

"A new world is in the making and requires the involvement of all: all have a part to play." *('The voice of Maitreya')*

THE ENTRY OF MAITREYA

"When, as now, man is at the crossroads, awaiting guidance on which direction to take, he sets up an invocative cry for help. Inevitably, when the cry has reached a certain pitch, We, your Elder Brothers, respond and answer. Thus is it today as men flounder wildly in the chaos of their own making, afraid to take the only steps which will save them from further chaos.

"Into this maelstrom Maitreya is about to enter, fully aware of the task which lies ahead. Only a Being of His immeasurable wisdom could accept such a burden. Only someone of His incomparable courage could undertake such a task.

"Out of the anarchic conditions of the present must He construct the new and better order. Out of the agony of millions must He fashion a new world.

"Who is there to help Him in His work of salvage?

"Who would rally to His cause and aid their brothers and sisters?

"Now, as never before, is the opportunity to serve a world in labour, a new world waiting to be born." *(The Master —, from 'The entry of Maitreya', SI, December 2001)*

This is the chance for everybody to serve the world as never in their history because the problems of today, and the change from this problematic world into the new world, the New Age, will never be repeated. There will be new ages, but this is a crisis point in the history of humanity and the world. So we, those of us who have shown our concern in various ways, should remember that the time is short to pull out everything we have, every ounce of strength, concentration and enthusiasm for the task of speaking to the world, to make known the fact of the presence of Maitreya, the presence of certain Masters, the eventual externalization of the work of a large section of the Masters.

"The Great Lord seeks to invest each individual life with sanctity and worth." *('The entry of Maitreya')*

One of the tragedies of today is that literally millions and millions of people have no sense of their own worth. They do not count, and they know they do not count. They know that their lives are insignificant and little better than animals. Their consciousness is not allowed to grow; their awareness is limited. They live to work, if they are lucky enough to have work, work which is usually mechanical and hard and simply muscle work for a pittance, for barely enough to keep their families in food. That is the reality for countless millions in the world. Remember that China has a billion people, that India has almost as many, perhaps 850 to 900 million, and South America, Africa, and other parts of the world have millions of people who live stunted and unpleasant lives. They do not count. They have no position in society. They have no voice in their own lives or futures. They are just pawns, barely existing as human beings, exploited and poor in every sense of the word. Poor in experience, poor in a material sense.

Maitreya "seeks to invest each individual life with sanctity and worth". To bring each person to the experience that he or she is a soul in incarnation, that they count, that every soul counts, that there is not a soul separate from any other soul. That everyone, whatever their condition now, should have, and will have, an equal right to education, food, shelter, healthcare, and the fulfilment of their full potential as living souls.

When that happens, when people have a sense of themselves as souls and of their own worth, that they count, their self-esteem can grow and become a creative force in their lives, and the world will be transformed. If you think of the endowment of talent, of resources, of millions and millions of lives who today are undernourished, underestimated and condemned to the lowest possible existence, you can imagine, then, the transformation which will occur on this Earth.

This is probably the most important thing that Maitreya comes to do. To endow millions and millions of people with a sense of their own worth, their self-esteem and the fact that they count, that everybody on Earth is here for a purpose. That purpose comes with the fact that they are a soul, that it is the soul's purpose that they are here, and that everybody is embarked on a journey, an adventure, open to all of us, but which is denied to the vast majority of people today as a conscious experience.

We middle-class people, living well, enjoying cultured and enriching experience from our lives, have little sense of the deprivation, the lack of awareness and hope which condemns millions of people to endless poverty and unworthy death. Maitreya is the only person in the world who could bestow on these millions the sense of self-worth, the self-esteem without which nobody can create anything worthwhile. You can imagine the change which will occur when these millions are contributing to the wealth and happiness, the culture and the richness of ideas which is about to change the world.

"He seeks to rid the world of violence and war. Where will He find His helpers? Who are ready to respond? Who have the courage to aid the Lord of Love? He knows already those on whom He can depend." *('The entry of Maitreya')*

Maitreya knows probably everything of any importance in the world and, of course, He has to know those on whom He can depend. He has to know those who already in their lives have signalled their readiness to work with Him for the restoration of the world.

Sitting here in our clover, in our comfort, well fed, it is

very difficult for us to feel the change which will blossom in most of the people in the world. There are 6.5 billion people in incarnation and we in the West make up only a third of that, perhaps 2 billion. Millions, two-thirds of the population, are hampered to a greater or lesser degree in doing what we take for granted. That is something which we have to keep uppermost in our minds. Because if we do not, we work always (whether we believe it or not, recognize it or not) from the complacency which is at the root of the whole problem.

People say money is the root of all evil. Maitreya says, no, nothing of the kind. Money is just an energy. It can be used for good and it can be used for evil.

The real evil, the fundamental cause of all the problems of the world today — the fact that two-thirds of the world live in absolute poverty, on less than a dollar a day, while others have not even that, and are dying in the millions — the root of all of that is our complacency. If we were not complacent we could not bear to live in a world in which these events were happening, these people were dying in the midst of plenty. We would not allow it to happen if we were not complacent. This is something which we need to remember and need to pass on, to make a fundamental part of any talk or lecture that we give, because this is the root of all the troubles in the world.

It is a sign of our separateness. Complacency results from separation — the sense that we are separate and that by competition we become superior — and that superiority allows us to live what we call 'well'. But we cannot live 'well' when two-thirds of the world are living and dying in absolute poverty. It is not possible to do so with impunity, and we do not. The result is crime. The result is catastrophe of one kind or another — governments which create wars for oil, for example. That is a catastrophe, and it is only possible because we are complacent, because we do not acknowledge the needs of millions of people who cannot take for granted what we take for granted: regular food, leisure, education and healthcare.

This is the real basis for working with the Christ. If anything is important, that is important. Only those who can suffer with those who suffer can experience, truly, the power and the love of the Christ. And He knows already those who can respond. They are those who are altruistic, who are the opposite of complacent, who are aware and engaged in life in every sense of the word. Not only their own little life, but the life of the world; not just with their family and friends, but with the world of six-and-a-half billion people, two-thirds of whom are living in absolute poverty. These are the people that Maitreya can call on, who recognize this and are burning to change it.

"His mantram is: fear not! All, in time, will be renewed. All, in time, will be returned to the Light." *('The entry of Maitreya')*

"His mantram is: fear not!" What a mantram! Nothing so inhibits humanity as fear. Fear would seem to be intrinsic to the human condition and yet from the point of view of the Masters it need not be. People are literally filled with fear. Fear is inculcated in every child from the earliest age and that conditioning feeds the fears which surround every individual, almost, in life. I do not know the proportion of those who fear and those who do not, but the number of people who do not know fear must be tiny indeed. Yet the mantram of Maitreya is: fear not!

If you fear you become useless, you are so inhibiting yourself that you are afraid to act. If you are afraid to act because you are afraid of change, you are afraid of what will happen if you act. That is the state of humanity today. We know that wars could be ended. We know that, but we allow them to take place because we are afraid.

I am absolutely amazed that the United Nations allowed Mr Bush to attack Iraq and Afghanistan. I cannot imagine how Mr Blair could align himself with that. Mr Blair is an intelligent man, a lawyer, a Prime Minister who had a huge follow-ing which he has thrown away for an ambition to be the prince of the world. If Mr Bush is king of the world, king of the cas-tle, Blair is the prince. If Bush is the chief man, the king, head of the biggest, strongest, wealthiest and most influential coun-try in the world, and if he, Blair, joins up with that and is seen to have a special relationship with Bush and America, then he is the prince, next in line. Such is the glamour, the illusion.

"Into your unhappy world now steps Maitreya. He knows your agony and suffering better even than you do yourselves, for He knows, too, the joy which is your birthright." *('The entry of Maitreya')*

That is the tragedy. Maitreya and the Masters see the joy which is the birthright of all humanity, that there is no need for the pain and suffering that is largely brought on by ourselves — if not from karma, then from the wrong governments which we elect if we are democratic, or from the wrong actions of tyrants and unholy men who seize power over the people.

This leaves humanity in a terrible state: dreaming of peace, dreaming of what could be done next year to the house, to the fields, how we might sow this, and how we might do that. If only we had a little money, we could transform this little patch of land, and we could maybe have another child and maybe life would be good, maybe it would be.

There are millions, literally millions, of men and women all over the world who think like that, who just need a little more money to do something tiny, a little improvement to a ramshackle shed of a house, or to enlarge their smallholding to grow just a little more, and maybe they could sell some of it and make a little more money and build up this tiny, little patch, this little smallholding which millions have but which are too small to feed their families.

Joy, which is our birthright, is in the mind of Maitreya all the time. If you could see into the heart of Maitreya, you

35

would see the pain, the suffering, the terrible agony of count-less millions, their cries, their longing, sometimes for death, for a better life, for more love, more ability, education, more knowledge of how to feed their families. Millions are in that position, and day by day they are filled with anguish and suf-fering that we with our little troubles rarely know. These are ongoing sufferings which most people in the West never ex-perience. Yet they are the common experience of two-thirds of the world's population. That is what Maitreya sees. That is the conscious awareness, moment to moment, of Maitreya. If you could see into His life, you would see that in His heart; He carries it around with Him.

At the same time He carries with Him His sense of joy, His joy as a Master, as a Divine Being Whose nature is joy, and these two things sit simultaneously in His experience. He knows that the pain, the agony of most people in the world could be changed very simply with just a little more: a little more food, a little more money, a little more building material or whatever their need.

"That joy would He restore to you in full and perfect meas-ure. For that is He among you." *('The entry of Maitreya')*

He comes to show us how to be ourselves as souls, and the nature of the soul is joy, endless, unfettered joy. What stands in the way of the manifestation and the experience of joy is our fear, our fear of life, our fear of death, our fear of everything that might change what we know. The fear of change fills hu-manity, and at the same time we all have a longing for change, for betterment. But how do we know the change is for the bet-ter? That is the rub. Not change just for the sake of it. We want change that is better, and people run away from change if they do not know that it will be better. Maitreya's task is to show humanity that the change they are longing for is for the better. That change will transform the lives of the vast majority of people in the world.

There are, of course, a lot of very rich, very powerful people who will not benefit — in that way — from the experience of Maitreya, who see that the coming of Maitreya is a warning sign for them, and who will fight bitterly to keep the manifestation of Maitreya out of common knowledge, and out of the life that they know. It is happening now; it has been happening for years.

It is not without cause that it has taken 30 years for this information to spread widely enough that today 30 million people have heard the story of the Reappearance of the Christ. Of 30 million, about 20 million have an open-minded expectation that it might be true, they look forward to it, they would like it to be true. They cannot bring themselves to say it is true because they do not have that conviction, but they have an open-minded sense that it would be wonderful if it were. Those who really believe it and work for it, for whom it is a reality, are about 2 million people. It is a lot of people, but compared with the population of the world it is very few, indeed, but enough.

Maitreya said long ago in the Agni Yoga books: "There was a time when ten true men could save the world. Then came a time when ten thousand was not enough. I shall call on one billion." Five or six years ago, I asked my Master: "Does Maitreya have His billion people yet?" He said: "One-and-a-half billion." He has by now well over one-and-a-half billion people ready to respond to His call for sharing and justice in the world. It does not have to be every single person but a proportion of people that create the same conviction in hundreds and then thousands and then millions of other people, that pertinent critical mass which one-and-a-half billion exceeds. Maitreya is in no doubt about humanity's response.

"Take Him to your hearts and let Him serve you. Know Him as your friend and Brother of Old. Let Him guide you and teach you; thus will you grow in your divinity.

"The time has come when you shall see His face. His smile of love will beckon you to His side. You will find your love magnified a thousandfold and, giving it in service to His Cause, enter into the Plan of which you are a part." *('The entry of Maitreya')*

Everyone in this room has taken incarnation at this time in order to serve the Plan in one way or another, mostly in the immediate sense of preparing the way for Maitreya. This is a fact known to most of you, but perhaps not to all of you.

THE GREAT LORD EMERGES

What will be the result of Maitreya's coming into the world? Interesting to speculate. But one result will be:

"Passports will become a thing of the past. In the coming time, people will be free to enter and to leave any country at will. So great will be the trust engendered by Maitreya's presence that all doors will be open, and a great and enriching interchange of peoples will take place. Thus, men will learn to know and to love their brothers, seeing them as little different from themselves." *(The Master —, from 'The Great Lord emerges', SI, June 1988)*

Is that not extraordinary? You do not have to be searched. You do not have to take your shoes off. You do not have to go through that guillotine-like affair, with the X-ray. You just go on, show your ticket, if you even need a ticket.

"Within weeks (this was written some time ago), Maitreya's open mission will begin, drawing to Him those who care and wish to serve the world with full heart. Those around and close to Him will prepare the ground, outlining His precepts and teaching. When a certain saturation has been achieved He Himself will enter the world's stage.

"Already the policies of nations are being reshaped by His influence. Already, many in high positions know of His presence and await His Announcement. Thus does He work quietly, affecting, under karmic law, the future of the race.

"The future holds for man unbelievable promise. From the Day of Declaration will begin a process which will transform this world, and take men to the highest levels of achievement.

"On that day, men and women everywhere will experience the love nature of God and know it as their own. Through their hearts will flow Maitreya's Ray, evoking from them an understanding altogether new. Sharing and Justice will be His call, and, thus guided and inspired, men will respond in full measure, remaking the world under His wise counsel.

"Not for nothing has He waited till now to make His appearance. Only now are men taking steps to put their house in order. Thus only now can He come forward and lead.

"On the Day of Declaration, He will outline the future for man, showing the alternatives which face the race today. Man's choice, He will show, can only be for sharing, for none other can sustain the planet longer." *('The Great Lord emerges')*

We, the developed world, that is, one-third of the world's population, misuse and denude the planet of resources and are making the world untenable. The world cannot sustain much longer the methods of husbandry of the Western nations today, with the most terrible result, the pollution which covers the world, the air, the land, the rivers, even the oceans. We destroy huge areas of what were once forests which supply, or did supply, the oxygen we need to live. We are making this planet uninhabitable. Even if sharing the world's resources was not a problem, it would, inevitably, be impossible for the world to carry on much longer with the present misuse of resources. We have to share in order that all can live, but we have to learn to live more simply so that we can all live. We have to simplify our lifestyles and make fewer and more intelligent demands on the planet. The ecological balance of the world will be one of Maitreya's main concerns, and He will from the highest level show the misuse of planet Earth and the inevitable results of continuing as we are. The need for action in that regard will become obvious to scientists, and through them, the governments of the world. To some extent, of course, this is already happening, but not enough.

"Men should know that all are needed to overcome the evils of the past. Division and separation have ancient roots and will not easily relinquish their hold. Each one, therefore, should see it as their task to aid the Christ in His work of transformation, giving of their best to reconstruct the world.

"Soon the world will know of the Splendour in its midst. Soon will men weep for joy at His appearance.

"Soon, too, will they take upon themselves the task of succour, re-establishing the true unity of men. Thus will it be. Thus will men know, at last, that Brotherhood which they long have cherished but till now were unable to find." *('The Great Lord emerges')*

ACTIONS OF AMERICA AND ISRAEL

You may think we are not going forward, in fact that we are going backwards. Every time there is a calamity like 9/11 or the attack on Iraq or something like that, we feel we are going backwards. People write to me and say: "Will this affect the coming out of Maitreya? Has it put back His coming?" In fact the answer is always, no. These events are not nothing, and they do have their impact on humanity; 9/11 has had an impact on America such as no event that I can think of in its recent history. This is quite extraordinary because 9/11 was an attack on one building in one city and another building in another city, so two buildings — the Twin Towers in New York and the Pentagon in Washington, and a proposed but thwarted attack on the White House — happened in no time at all, in one morning. Over 3,000 people were killed, which is a huge number — but not when compared with the loss of life in all the previous terrorist attacks on America abroad, in Britain from the IRA, from ETA in Spain for years. Not compared with continuous terror attacks, month in and month out for years; constant attacks, which you can get used to if they are not completely destructive, if they do not destroy some vital part of the daily life of the people involved.

But 9/11 seems to have had an extraordinary psychological impact on the people of America, and this has been worked up, magnified out of all proportion, by the present administration. So you have not been allowed to forget it, just as the Israelis make the Holocaust — an unbelievably terrible happening — something which humanity must on no account ever forget. They have raised it as a great symbol of their pain and suffering, allowing them any excess in relation to the Palestinians. Jewish people everywhere — rightly, because of what happened to so many Jewish people before Israel was created — have lived daily in the remembrance of that event when 6 million Jews died in the death camps of Germany. But so did millions of other people: Gypsies, Poles, Hungarians, Romanians and Russians died in the same way, in the same places. We do not hear these laments from the Russians or the Poles or the Gypsies, from the people of Romania or any of the Eastern European countries.

I am not trying to diminish the importance or the horror of the death camps, but humanity cannot go on forever holding them up as an illustration of how horrible humanity can be to itself. That, I think, is a profound mistake on the part of the Jewish people and the Israeli government in particular, so that the world will never see their experience as other than through the eyes of their own self-pity. It prevents them from seeing the reality of their own intolerance and intransigence in relation to the people of Palestine. Of all the people in the world who have suffered, suffered over centuries, the Jewish people probably win the prize; but in Palestine it does not seem to count for anything. The Holocaust is used by Israel, even unconsciously, to justify the oppression of the Palestinians in a way which is heartless and has profound danger for the world as a whole.

Americans wonder why people hate them. Well, after 9/11 people loved America. After 9/11 the world was filled with sympathy and warm feelings for the people of America because they had lost up to 3,000 people. They were not all Americans, of course, but up to 3,000 people died at a stroke in the Twin Towers, but the government has manipulated the situation and created 'a war against terrorism' as a result. There can never be a war against terrorism, which is worldwide, not a State or country. It is a fantasy, but it gives this government the right to make war on whichever country they feel is aiding and abetting terrorist activity.

They are aiding and abetting terrorist activity themselves. They support Israel to the tune of £3 billion a year just for armaments, so that the Israeli army is the most powerful in the area, and one of the most powerful in the whole world. It has the nuclear bomb. No one thinks it should not have a nuclear bomb. Why was Iraq not allowed to have a nuclear bomb? Why should Iraq not have weapons of mass destruction if Israel is allowed to have weapons of mass destruction? One of the reasons given by the present American administration for attacking Iraq was that it had 19 resolutions against it from the United Nations which have not been carried out. Israel has 63 resolutions against it which have not been carried out. Why? Because America has a veto in the Security Council and will not allow the resolutions to go further.

That is the kind of government, I am afraid, that is in power in America. It is a power which aids and abets the oppression of the Palestinians while at the same time pretending, going through the motions of helping, to set up a state of Palestine within the Israeli State.

The best proposal that has been offered to Palestinians for a solution to their problem and the creation of a Palestinian State was put forward at the Camp David agreement and was rejected by Mr Arafat — rightly so, because it was unfair and unjust and would not have lasted for that very reason. Nothing will last which is basically unjust and unfair, because the people will inevitably revolt against it. Maitreya advised Mr Arafat not to sign the agreement. That is one of the reasons — there are many — why Mr Sharon hates, loathes, Mr Arafat, and why the Americans have tried to sideline Mr Arafat and get a Prime Minister in his place. [Speaking in 2004.]

It is not possible for the Palestinians to sign an agreement which gives them something like 40 per cent of their homeland. The West Bank belonged, until the pre-emptive attack by Israel in 1967, to the King of Jordan. Maitreya asked King Hussein of Jordan (at the Conference which Maitreya held in April 1990 in London) if he would give up sovereignty of the West Bank for it to become a homeland for the Palestinian people. The good King of Jordan, now dead, agreed to the proposal, and so the West Bank became the possible homeland, with the Gaza Strip, for the Palestinians.

Since then it has been whittled away by the building of settlements by the Israelis over much of the West Bank. They are huge conglomerations of buildings with walls and a little army round them to keep them secure, and roads built throughout the West Bank connecting them. These divide up the West Bank, until what is offered the Palestinian people is about 40 per cent of the original land. That is the reality, and that is why Maitreya advised Mr Arafat not to sign the agreement. That was the best proposal that there has been. The building of settlements has gone on and on. They have completely decimated the West Bank, cutting off the Palestinians from their land, their orchards, making it impossible for them to earn a living.

Now they are building the wall. That is done coldly, professionally, in response to what they call the terrorism of the people of Palestine who are using the only methods they have to get any redress, or a semblance of the freedom which Israel wants for itself.

The early Israelis taught the Palestinians about terrorism. Israel was formed by terrorism. There were a number of gangs, like the Stern gang and the Irgun Zeva'i Le'umi. They fought as terrorists against the British and the Palestinians, and 'won' the area we know as Israel. They fought and wrestled for that land just as the Palestinian people are fighting to hold onto the little bit of land that they could call home. It is so unfair, and it has the weight of the American government and the strength of the American dollar and army behind it. There will never be peace in the world while that situation pertains. If there is no peace in Palestine, there will be no peace in the world as a whole.

The war in Iraq is part of a wider war in the Middle East between two opposing forces, the forces of light and the forces of darkness, or evil. The forces of evil have replicated themselves from the Axis Powers in the war from 1939 to 1945. There are three such points of deep evil in the present situation. One is in this country, America, centred in the Pentagon; one is in Israel; and one is in Eastern Europe. These three points make a triangle which potentizes all the energy which is sent through them.

This is the same energy — although luckily at a lower potency — as drove Hitler, Mussolini, and the groups around them, and the warmongers in Japan, from 1939 to 1945. It is the energy of the forces of evil on this planet. It is not less than that. The Masters have said it will take all the strength and awareness of humanity, plus that of Hierarchy itself, to contain. It will be contained, but in the meantime Israel is making mischief, terrible menace, in the Middle East, and America is waging the same mischief in Iraq and Afghanistan, and is ready to do the same wherever the 'need' arises.

One of the occult happenings of great importance for us to be aware of is that a large number of the German forces — army, SS troops, a few majors, lieutenant generals — have reincarnated in Israel, and many of them are behind the events which are taking place in Palestine today. Sharon is an old terrorist from the early days of Israel, and there are a number like him, about his age, who were terrorists then. They fought and terrorized to make the state of Israel. Now they accuse the Palestinians of terrorism, which they learned from the Israelis. The Palestinians have nothing else, no other means, because they are not allowed by the Israelis to have an army, any weapons besides their home-made guns, and what they can smuggle in from Egypt. It is a very unfair situation and supported to the hilt by the present US administration.

Their time will come. This is the end time of those dealing in end times.

THE RECEPTION OF MAITREYA

"As Maitreya's approach comes ever nearer, let us look more closely at the likely reactions to His presence. In the first place, those who have worked to make known that presence may be surprised to find the reactions of many more muted than they envisaged." *(The Master —, from 'The reception of Maitreya', SI, October 2001)*

That is people like you around the world, those who have been engaged for years and years in making known His presence, may be surprised to find the reactions of many to be more muted than they envisaged.

"Initially, this may well be so. In starting His open mission, the Great Lord must tread carefully, not to frighten away those He seeks to help." *('The reception of Maitreya')*

45

If Maitreya came out and started speaking like I do, nobody would listen. It would be too upsetting, nobody would recognize Him as the Christ or Maitreya or any big figure at all, but just as a man who has got a 'bee in his bonnet'.

"Therefore, a quiet note, but heartfelt, should be looked for. In time, a greater urgency and force of statement will be appropriate." *('The reception of Maitreya')*

I can say what I like, but Maitreya will be speaking not to invited audiences, but on television, on radio and so on. So it is important that He does not make people turn away.

"In time, a greater urgency and force of statement will be appropriate, and trenchant, indeed, will be His call to men. Expect, therefore, a growing emphasis, a sterner warning, from Maitreya's lips." *('The reception of Maitreya')*

"Tell about the lies!" He says, shouting out: "Tell them about the lies! Show out the lies! Show out the lies!" A couple of the group members in the US were giving a talk recently and Maitreya and the Master Jesus were sitting there (in disguise), although they did not know at the time. The co-workers were answering questions, and one of them was saying: "They are …" (he hesitated, not liking to use the word) and either Maitreya or the Master Jesus said: "Go on, say it! Say the word!" He still hesitated. "Say it!" They urged him, "Fascists, fascists!" Maitreya will speak directly, but not at first. A quiet note, but heartfelt, and then a greater urgency, more vividly.

"As time proceeds, His thoughts will find response of differing kind. Those more traditionalist will find many of His ideas difficult to embrace, and will denounce them in strident terms. Others, less hidebound, will consider and appraise them, and from this group will He find many who will gladly espouse His cause. In growing numbers, they will gravitate to Him and lend their voice to His counsel.

"Proceeding thus, Maitreya's teaching will draw forth from men their highest aspiration, awakening them to the troubles and perils of this time; and also to the simple means of conquering for ever the problems and dangers of today. Thus will it be. Thus will men receive the insight and the leadership they yearn for, and thus will they call for the changes so sorely needed to the fabric of men's lives.

"Of course, it is only to be expected that many will oppose the teaching of the Great Lord. Religious groups, deeply embedded in their own doctrines and expectations, will strongly disavow Maitreya's presence and ideas, and many unpleasant accusations will be directed towards Him." *('The reception of Maitreya')*

I was called "the beast" the other night on a radio phone-in. "I can hear the breath of the beast behind you, George." George Noory was the interviewer and said: "You do not sound like a beast."

"Nevertheless, many will be inspired and renewed in faith, and will give of their best for Maitreya's Cause.

"The business conglomerate, so highly invested in today's crumbling structures, will react in one of two ways: those who see Maitreya as the enemy of all they stand for will oppose and thwart His counsel to their utmost effort. Those who see Him as the voice of the future, as the only possible way for men, will welcome and espouse His ideas, and lend their expertise to His growing support." *('The reception of Maitreya')*

That will be, probably, about one-third for Him and two-thirds against Him in the business world, so it is a lot of people.

"Thus will the factions act and take their stand: for or against the future, the only way open to men.

"The masses everywhere will follow their leaders. Gradually they will realize that Maitreya speaks for them, their needs, their aspirations for a better, safer life for their families, a future they can dimly feel is theirs by right, waiting to be born. Then will the world's peoples raise their voices in support and praise of the Great Lord, and call on His teaching to enlighten and ennoble them, and to lead them willingly into that beckoning and blessed future." *('The reception of Maitreya')*

So it will be. People will take their stand. The great Sword of Cleavage will act and separate those who are ready for the future, ready to change, ready to make a world in which all people can live decent lives, at a simpler level, but a level that all will find more attractive, more worthwhile. And those who see an end to their privilege, their power, their money, their facility to get more money and therefore more power; they will see that this is not the way for them. They will oppose Him, and there are those now who oppose Him.

MAITREYA HASTENS TO EMERGE

"Many today would be amazed by the prospect which We, your Elder Brothers, see for man. Despite the hazards and tensions, the crises and alarms, We know that men will rise above them and create the New Time. We know that the time of testing is all but over, that a watershed has been surmounted, and that man stands at the threshold of discoveries beyond his imagining.

"We see, indeed, the problems which men face. We know the apprehension which kills the joy in many human hearts. We share the pain and agony of countless millions living and dying in despair.

"We know that despite the dangers and injustice, the spirit of hope is ever ready to rise and inspire the loftiest deeds, for it is the divine in man and is unquenchable.

"'The deepest dark is just before the dawn' goes the old adage, and thus it is today for men. Amid the chaos and fear, the perplexity and pain, We see the resolution and the end of conflict, the glow of the light which will awaken men to the promise of the future.

"All works under Law and a new state of equilibrium is being created by Us. Appearances notwithstanding, a new rhythm asserts itself and will bring into balance this discordant world.

"Maitreya Himself wields this mighty Law and brings its cosmic origin to the affairs of men. Thus will new hope arise in men and thus will they take the steps to reshape their future in accordance with the Plan." *(The Master —, from 'Maitreya hastens to emerge', SI, September 2002)*

The Master is talking, of course, about the Spirit of Peace or Equilibrium Whose energy is now the most powerful in the whole world. Not the most powerful per se, but the most prevalent in the world. There is more of that tremendous cosmic energy functioning and acting and changing events in the world than any other of the tremendous energies which Maitreya releases.

The Spirit of Peace or Equilibrium, as many of you will know, works with the Law of Action and Reaction which are opposite and equal. The effect of this energy is to transform the prevalent hatred, violence and crisis, alarm and tension, into its opposite. So we shall enter into an era of peace and tranquillity, of mental and emotional poise, in exact proportion to the existing violence and hatred, turmoil and discord.

Through the work of the great Law of Action and Reaction, that mighty Avatar, Who overshadows Maitreya in a way very similar to the way He overshadowed Jesus in Palestine, daily creates the conditions of the future. These energies have yet to come down onto the physical plane in great potency, but they are transforming the world even now. That is why the Masters and Maitreya are so hopeful. It is a hope based, of course, on knowledge.

THE AVATAR

"... millions now stand ready to receive the Teacher." *(The Master —, from 'The Avatar', **SI**, October 1988)*

That is interesting. "Knowingly or not", the Master says, millions now stand ready to receive the Teacher. Thirty million people have heard this story, 20 million have an open-minded expectancy that it could be true, and 2 million people are convinced that this is so.

"All now conspires to bring about this blessed event. Cosmic and planetary, the Forces of Regeneration reap now the harvest of Their sowing and bring into being the condition which allows Maitreya to appear. Forced by force of law to withhold, for a time, His open mission, He knows that the law is being fulfilled, the debts are being paid, the opportunities taken; and that now in full splendour may He appear, and receive the love and service which, many will avow, they are ready to bestow on Him.

"His Grace already does embrace the world. His Love enfolds the nations, East and West, North and South. None escape the arrow of His Love.

"Daily, His Ray awakens men to their true destiny, and conjures anew their hope and trust.

"From far and wide the representatives of the people gather at His side, and He endows them with a wisdom altogether new. Soon, this enlightened group of men and women will present their story and experience, and prove past all gainsaying that the Christ is in our midst. Millions then will hearken to this promise and demand to see the Representative of God. Under many names will He then come forward and thus fulfil the hopes of every faith." *('The Avatar')*

I called Him the Christ because He embodies the Christ Principle, but of course, Muslims await Him as the Imam Mahdi, Jews as the Messiah, Hindus as Krishna, Buddhists as Maitreya Buddha (they have His name right). All of these are names for one and the same individual, which will be an extra problem for humanity, a problem and a surprise and a source of joy in the end because when they see Him they will know it is the Imam Mahdi, the Christ or Maitreya Buddha or Miroko Bosatsu, or whichever the name of the Being they await. It will be a tremendous experience for humanity.

These representatives of the people, people whom Maitreya has already trained in meetings and endows with "a wisdom altogether new", this group of enlightened men and women will present their story, they will talk about Him, that they have met Him, that they know Him and that they can vouch for His origin from whatever point of view they express it. This will have a tremendous effect on the masses of people.

"His call for Justice, Peace, and Brotherhood will then be heard among the nations, avowing God's concern for the well-being of men everywhere. His voice will remind the peoples of their origin and destiny, and bring them, in trust, to the feet of God.

"That His task is well prepared you may be sure. His disciples, inwardly trained, have long engaged themselves in this work of preparation and know well their various roles. Called into action, they will carry the work of reconstruction to every corner of the world and replace misery with joy, separation with unity, hatred and malice with altruistic love. Thus will it be. Thus will the New Time enter its course of splendour, and thus will mankind realize the promise which His presence brings.

"That not all will testify to His Glory is certain; for some, the Mantle of God has too brilliant a light. But most will see in Him the fulfilment of their hopes and dreams for justice and love, for sanity and freedom. And to Him will they turn their eyes and hearts, seeking guidance and comfort, inspiration and purpose, enlightenment and love. These in abundance will He bestow upon the world. A vast River of Truth is He, nurturing all who from these waters deeply drink. A Fountain of Love is He, enclosing all within His heart. An Avatar like none before is He, come to lead men into the realization that they, too, are Gods." *('The Avatar')*

* The quotations from the Master —, through Benjamin Creme, first published in *Share International (SI)* magazine, are also published in the book *A Master Speaks* (third expanded edition, 2004).

** For a list of Maitreya's appearances, see Appendix to *The Great Approach.*

*** *Share International*, April 2003.

QUESTIONS AND ANSWERS

THE IMMINENCE OF MAITREYA'S EMERGENCE

Q. Why did the Master suggest the Reappearance of the Christ as the subject for your lecture now (after all those years of making this information known)? Is it to do with the imminence of Maitreya's public emergence at this time?

A. Yes, of course. The Master has been writing these articles [in *Share International* magazine for the last 23 years] about Maitreya's emergence and the response to it and all the intricacies of work that go into the creation of this extraordinary happening. The articles were grouped, sometimes in twos or threes dealing with similar ideas or themes, and then again talking about other subjects. It is the way the Master works, and it is very similar to the way Maitreya worked in the 140 messages which He gave through me and which can be found in the book *Messages from Maitreya, the Christ*.

Maitreya would deal with a subject: the emergence, poverty, the idea of sharing, and so on. He would talk about it two or three times in different ways, bringing all the facets together to give a complete picture. Then He would take up another theme for a number of weeks. Later He would go back, perhaps, to the first theme and deal in even more depth with it and add facets that would never have occurred to us but which expanded its meaning.

When the Masters, however spontaneous They are, and They are certainly spontaneous, are presenting a body of teachings or information, They tend to see it as a whole and take each idea separately and look at it in depth — every aspect of it — and then drop it, take up another idea, and do the same there. So They cover an enormous range.

Q. The Master's articles seem alternately to highlight the dire state of the planet, and then the progress being made under the stimulus of the Masters. Which is the stronger trend in the world now?

A. The stronger trend in the world now is the progress being made under the stimulus of the Masters. It is true, the Master does this. He writes an article that is all about the dire state of the planet, the problems, but He always ends on a positive note. He always brings hope at the end of it. "Despite the exigencies of the time, despite the terror, the famine, all these inequities that abound in the world, nevertheless, the world is more ready for the Christ than it has ever been."

They were not ready for the Christ 2,000 years ago, so He could only stay three years. This time He is going to stay 2,500 years and stimulate the transformation of the world. It will be a very interesting time indeed.

If you took all the articles, marked them off and counted them, you would find the stronger emphasis is on the progress being made, the great changes already under way. The changes that have taken place normally would take 100 years, yet they have happened in 10 years, sometimes almost overnight.

An example is the end of apartheid in South Africa. Can you imagine how long apartheid lasted in the US, how established that was? Yet now, not every black man in America feels safe or accepted, especially in the south, but compared with even 40 or 50 years ago — the mid 1950s for instance, a terrible time, the McCarthy era — you have an extraordinary transformation. Likewise in South Africa, it is a different situation altogether.

THE TIMING OF MAITREYA'S EMERGENCE

Q. Isn't this a difficult time for Maitreya to come forward?
A. It is obvious that the choice of this theme, 'the Reappearance of the Christ', after all these years must mean that the time has now become ripe when Maitreya will come out and

begin His task. We may think this is a terrible moment for Maitreya, and in some ways it is. To meet with people who are receptive and who can listen and put into practice what He is talking about is one thing, but to come on radio and television with sceptical interviewers, is something else again. Not that He is frightened by scepticism. Not at all. It could hardly be the case.

In the beginning it might be quite difficult even for someone like Maitreya Who not only knows the answers to all the questions that would be asked, but Who knows which questions to put into the mind of the person who is asking. So the interviewer might find himself asking questions that he had no intention of asking. He will have some questions written down but some other question might come out. So perhaps it might not be so difficult as all that.

Nevertheless, it is a huge world out there with very many different countries, different systems and ways of thinking even about the same things, different values placed on these things.

He will not be called Maitreya at first. So, if the interviewer is a wise person, he might think this is somebody extraordinary, especially when he finds himself asking questions that he did not intend to ask. So Maitreya knows the answers to His own questions.

People have often asked me, how will it be? He has got to talk to the world about all these things and just how can He get it over? As the Master says, and I think it is very telling, these groups like yourselves who have been doing this work, somewhat, over the years may be disappointed; you will be somewhat surprised, anyway, at the quietness of His approach, the lack of emphasis or the loss of an opportunity — you might think — to bring in all the 'big guns'.

Maitreya will be concerned with making His appearances as often as possible. In the beginning, of course, it is more difficult, but He has His ways and means. His appearances will become more and more frequent until He has a regular broadcast on television and radio around the world.

Q. Is Maitreya awaiting the best timing to go public even though He can come out today? What is holding Him back?
A. Maitreya is awaiting the best timing to go public. He is waiting for the best opportunity, that is timing, in which there will be the best and quickest acceptance of what He has to say.

There is still an enormous body of people in the world who do not want anything to do with Maitreya or His ideas. All the religious groups have their own fundamentalists who together make a huge block. Think of the fundamentalist Christians, the fundamentalist Muslims, the fundamentalist Jews, Hindus now, even Buddhists to some extent. It is a huge number of people, and they have to come to grips with this reality. They will not see Him as the Christ or the Imam Mahdi, not at first.

The best timing is when the crumbling economic system is bringing the West to its knees economically, and bringing it into reality for the first time. We have lived in unreality for so long. We think, and our leaders think, that we can go on in the old ways, exactly as we have done — more competition, more greed, more of the same, and it will just go on, we will win. It is not so any longer; it does not work.

If two-thirds of the world's population are living in poverty then the economic system does not work. If we think that they will go on without asking that it work for them, then we are sorely out of step with reality. Maitreya will make that clear.

An immediate collapse of the economic structures, a stock-exchange crash in Europe and America, would bring Maitreya forward right away. That would bring us into reality. That is one of the factors that He is waiting for, that sense of reality which it would bring about. We would see that it does not work. We thought it was working, it seemed to work for some of us, but through our complacency we did not even think of those for whom it does not work. One of Maitreya's major tasks is to throw cold water on this complacency, make it very uncomfortable to be complacent.

I can remember people coming to a meeting of mine and saying: "I thought this was going to be a message of hope, but I feel awful. I feel so unhappy. I feel so guilty and horrible." I said: "Jolly good. That is what we call love."

You have to cut through that complacency. If people only want to be, "Ah, lovely", it is not going to change the world. It is important that they know that the Christ is in the world and not alone, and that the world is ready for change and will change. But if they only want to be made to feel good, it is not going to help the world because they are not the people who are actually working in the world.

Q. Is Maitreya still waiting for the stock-market collapse?
A. Yes, He is still waiting for the stock-market crash, but if political events were sufficiently critical He would come out whether there was a stock-market crash or not — if He saw that His presence and what He has to say would have a powerful effect on the political situation.

Q. Are there any circumstances that would bring Him forward before that?
A. There are a number of crises that could bring Him forward, but He knows the Law and you can be sure He obeys the Law to the letter. Yet at the same time He knows how to manipulate that Law. He knows how much it may be manipulated and still be within the Law.

He will talk about the Karmic Law, about which He knows and understands more even than among His peers, even among the Masters, Who, we suppose, know about the niceties of the Karmic Law.

If there is an occurrence in which the peace of the world is threatened, Maitreya would act and come forward without the stock-market crash. It would have to be a very dangerous situation, and even then His action would have to not break the Karmic Law. He has to make these fine judgments, which are of cosmic level. He is dealing with cosmic energies.

It is not a simple, straight option. Everything He does has to take into account a thousand cosmic possibilities, those that are conducive to the act and possibilities that would be harmful if He carried out the act. It is a very fine and subtle judgment that He has to make all the time. His work is not simple at all. That is why I am trying to explain the complexity of the situation.

If there were a real danger to the world, the possibility of a conflagration on a world scale that would include the use of nuclear weapons, He could act. He would invoke, as I understand it, the energies that would defeat the process. Or it may be something altogether different. Not that the Masters would ever use force. There might be something that the Lords of Karma could be induced to do. That is also a possibility. But do not hold it strongly in your mind.

There are possibilities and impossibilities, but where the Masters are concerned, you cannot say they are impossible. You can always think things are possible. They are tremendously powerful, and I do not think anyone has an idea of just how powerful an Avatar Maitreya is. He is wielding energies that have never been wielded before in unison on this planet.

He is a tremendously powerful Being, and has to work within the Law in the use of that power. That is the only thing that restricts Him.

Q. Is a third world war imminent — what with the conflict in the Middle East?
A. No, it is not. If we were in a situation which was so 'hot'

— it is very 'hot' at present [as of August 2006] — that World War III was inevitable, Maitreya would intervene.

It is better that He does not have to intervene because it would infringe human free will. But if it were necessary, He would intervene. In that case, He would be restricted in what He can give to humanity for quite some time, until our karma allowed Him to give what He can give. If He used that karmic gift, as it were, to prevent a third world war, it would hinder Him from doing things that He otherwise would do.

The Masters, with a broader vision, know that eventually things will clarify and peace will be established. They know, as Maitreya says, that the end is known from the beginning. Have no fear. That does not mean sit still and do nothing. That is the point.

You have to be inspired to act. He says: "Nothing happens by itself. Man must act and implement his will." People, full of idealism, think that if you can envisage something, it already exists; that if you know that God is perfect, then the world is perfect. You cannot shut your eyes to all the ills in the world. It is foolish. It is not adult. Be adult and face the ills of the world and do something about them. You have to act to implement your will. If you want peace, justice, sharing and right relationship, you have to do it. Make it known that you want it. Elect the right people to get it. Act. Become active. Otherwise, you live in the clouds.

This is a time like none other in history. It will not be repeated. The Hierarchy of Masters is returning to the world for the first time in 98,000 years. You have the opportunity to work for Them, to make easier the work of Maitreya, to light the way, to make known to the world that He is here. Don't wait till Maitreya comes out in the open. Tell everybody who will listen that He is here, what His plans are, what His priorities are — right relationship, sharing, justice, peace — these are the priorities. Looking after the planet is a number one priority. You have to make these your own, not just listen to someone like me.

We all have to become involved and to tell the world what is happening in the world, that this is the most amazing time, there has never been a time in the history of the world like this time. To be alive at this time is an extraordinary blessing.

With all the pain and the suffering in the world the opportunity for humanity is immense.

Q. When you say that Maitreya is coming out soon do you mean an interview on television?
A. When I say coming out, the first will be an interview on American television, yes. This talk is an indication, you can take it from me, that Maitreya's emergence is, as the Master has so often put it, soon. Now you know what soon means after all. It is really very soon, sooner than you would like, probably. Do you think this work is going to get easier as it goes on, as Maitreya comes out? This is the easy time. It is going to become the opposite. You are going to be so much in action and caught up in argument and feel all the confrontation.

Q. Is Maitreya's message going to Africa?
A. Maitreya lives in London in various Hindu temples. He goes to the mosque and to churches, but He lives in temples. He lives for a few years in one temple and a few years in another. While He is in those temples, He teaches the swamis in the temples about His ideas for world transformation, then He sends them out around the world. They spread out around the world, giving the people part of their experience, the teachings of Maitreya. Maitreya's teachings are going out through these many swamis, very educated, intelligent men, brought up in the Hindu tradition. This goes on all the time. A lot of them go to Asia and parts

of Africa where there are Hindu communities who will need swamis in the temples.

SPIRITUAL CRISES

Q. You spoke of the need to frame the message so people can take it in, in the context of their experience. How might we more specifically approach this in a way that taps into people's soul instead of the usual fear-based approaches that are common in the grass roots activism arenas?

A. It is impossible to talk about the Reappearance of the Christ and the Masters without tapping into that person's soul, invoking the soul experience and intuition of the person you are speaking to. It is trial and error: you fail with some people and succeed with others. If you yourself try to work as a soul, if you try to see things from the point of view of the soul, it is not like seeing things in a mystical way. The soul is not mystical. It is a great mystery for most people, but it is not a mystical idea.

When people think of approaching things as a soul, they are inclined to think that is a very high, mystical-sounding approach. It is not. You can be, and should be, as practical as I am in putting forward this message. Some people come to my lectures and say: "I thought it was going to be about the Reappearance of the Christ. It is all about politics and economics." It is both. Politics and economics are spiritual ideas.

The current global crisis is a spiritual crisis. It is a crisis of Being. Humanity does not know who it is, what it is, where it comes from, where it is going. It is a spiritual crisis for the entire world. That spiritual crisis is focused today through the political and economic fields.

That is why we in the West have a total lack of concern. We know and yet put up with the fact that millions are dying in the East, in Africa, for lack of food which is rotting away in the storehouses of the Western world. That is a spiritual reality.

The fact that we can put up with that is a spiritual error. It is not just an error of common sense, an error of distribution or bookkeeping; as though we left them out of the equation and somehow the food did not get there. It is not that kind of error. It is the effect of a spiritual lack in us. We are not what we think we are. We think we are clever, intelligent, able to run our lives and the life of the country in ways that are beneficial for all. It is not true. You may be clever and intelligent. You may have good ideas. You may have the best of intentions. But unless you are spiritual in the real sense, in the practical sense, you will not handle those qualities, the cleverness, the intelligence, the thought for others. You will be complacent. You will think: "I am all right, we have done rather well here. What is wrong with our country? It is great. We have to make the odd war now and again just to teach a lesson to some upstart, but apart from that, we are fine" — forgetting that you are only one part of the world.

To be spiritual really means to take in the world as a whole, to think in global terms. This is needed above all at the present time. All governments should be under the pressure of the educated public to take the broader view, to see the necessity of having right human relationships in the political and economic sense, not just in a cosy, friendly, one-to-one human sense.

It is not either/or, of course. You need the cosy, friendly, one-to-one human sense as a matter of course. But also as a matter of course, Britain, France, America, Japan, all the developed nations, should have the same feelings towards the Africans and Indians, the people who are suffering, living on a dollar a day — one-fifth of the world's population. It is unbelievable. There are 1.3 billion people in the world living on a dollar a day. Of these, millions die daily, hourly, moment-to-moment, from starvation.

The fact that we allow that to happen is the spiritual crisis.

We tend to think of it only in economic and political terms. But the economic and political reality is the spiritual crisis. We have to see it from its core. The core is wrong human relationship. We tend not to know or put any emphasis on the fact that humanity is one.

There is only one humanity, one group called humanity, the human kingdom. It is not the only kingdom, not even the most important. We only think of one section of it, the developed world, as the important part of the important human kingdom.

From the Masters' point of view, the human kingdom is just one kingdom among others, highly important, but it is a part of the evolution of planet Earth. And planet Earth is a part of the evolution of the solar system, and so on, higher and higher. There is no break in it. There is no point where you could cut it down and say: "Let us stop there. This is America, let us just look after America." It is what America tends to do, look after America. It is what Britain tends to do, look after British interests. Is it in the British, American, French, Italian, Japanese, or in the Russian interest to do this?

We always put it into these specified local, not global, interests. There is no such thing as specifically American, Russian, or British interests. There are world interests, human interests, and unless these are solved, there will be no humans in the world. That is what we have to grasp and that is what you can put forth.

That is the soul talking. That is how the soul sees the world. When people see this, they say: "You know, you are right," because their soul is telling them it is right. They see it as a soul. But if you do not see it as a soul, you do not see it as a spiritual crisis, just an economic or political crisis. They are political and economic crises, but these are the fields in which the spiritual crisis is focused.

Q. Could you say more about the mechanism of complacency?
A. The mechanism of complacency is habit. You in America are born and brought up in a country which is so materialistic in its outlook that complacency is the inevitable result. You are so educated at school and by the media that America becomes the limit of your seeing, your imagination, your sense of the world. It is because America is so big. You have a powerful media service which day after day puts that which is happening in America at the forefront of your consciousness. At school in America you are brought up to salute the flag everyday. This does not happen everywhere. You would not get the national flag saluted by many school children. They would think you were daft. Yet you take it for granted. Also America is so rich compared with many countries that you easily feel in its materialistic atmosphere that you are all right and do not have to think about those abroad. As a young country, you also believe that people have to stand on their own feet and make of life what they can. There is much truth in this but carried to excess it leads to the complacency that threatens world peace.

America brings together a bit of Europe, just lifted over the seas — British, French, Dutch, German, Scandinavian, Spanish — and others from other parts of the world, Africans brought in as slaves. You get a melange which is unique, but it is a part of a Plan. You are part of a Plan. You are all here for a purpose quite apart from the Reappearance of the Christ.

You are here because there are three great experiments being carried out in the world — one here in America, one in Russia, and one in Britain. Here the experiment is to bring together these people, not from all over the world, but from Europe mainly. With a few exceptions they are brought into this big melting pot and allowed to melt together and to become whatever they become. You might have started off as half-Swedish and half-Scottish, and you end up after a few generations being partly Swedish, partly Scottish, partly Iranian or

64

Hungarian or whatever. It is a melange, a big melting pot. You are the cheese that comes out of the melt.

You are somebody else. You are Americans, something quite different from what you began. Eventually, out of this mix, will come a very distinct figure that will be American, unlike anything else.

Russia has another plan. The plan there is for a grouping of nations to come together. Russia is even more huge than the United States, one-sixth of the world's surface. There is Russia as we know it, up to about Moscow, and then as far as you can look from an aeroplane, as far east as you can go through country after country, and south to the Ukraine and all the different countries. All these were part of the Soviet Union, before it was broken up. Each is now an independent country, part of a federation of nations. That federation will be all these different people living together in harmony, eventually, not seeking to intermarry or fuse or blend as you are doing here.

In Britain the same is happening. The British Commonwealth, which used to cover the globe as colonies, now covers the globe as independent countries. We have a large population from the Commonwealth countries: from South Africa, from various states in east and west Africa, from all the states of the West Indies, a few from North and South America, and from India, Pakistan, Bangladesh and Sri Lanka. We gave Hong Kong back to the Chinese, but people come from Hong Kong to Britain just as they have always done. There is a large grouping of people from all over the world in Britain. In some towns, you would think you were in India. Every shop, every restaurant, is Indian, and it is much more colourful. It is a completely different atmosphere from the town next door, which is as British as they come.

This is a deliberate mixing of peoples of the world together, but not fusing or blending, being themselves, Indian, Pakistani, African, not isolated, but living together in clear separate groups, with their own religions, their own traditions, setting up shops, cafés and restaurants, and living in harmony. It is not pure harmony at the moment. The aim is that all of these representatives of a large part of the world should live together, learn to live together, in harmony. That is where Maitreya is, so it is easier perhaps for that to occur.

These three experiments are all to do with the grouping of peoples. One is a melange like here in America. That is one of the reasons why you have the problems of America. When you bring diverse people together in the numbers which happened in America, you are bound to end up with problems. But eventually the mixing will go on, the stirring of it will go on. The American Masters are stirring away.

It is a very interesting experiment. If you know this, it certainly answers a lot of the questions that come up about the nature of social life in different countries, even the look of people.

FREE WILL

Q. You have talked about leaders in various fields who have had contact with Maitreya and the Masters and have been prepared by Him. Why is their work not more evident in the present situation?

A. I wonder if that is true. How evident would you expect it to be? What is the area of your research? I do not know what you expect. There are people all over the world who know, like we know, that Maitreya is in the world and who know why He is here. They may not know all the esoteric background to His coming, but they know that a great Teacher is in the world and He could be, from their point of view, the Christ. They know He has very explicit ideas about the need for humanity to change, and in what direction, and that they can be of service in influencing the direction of that change. They know that, but they are not going to write it in the newspapers. They are not necessarily in France or Germany or Holland. They might be in South America; in fact they are in South America. They might be in China; they are in China and Russia.

We in Europe tend to think that everything of any importance happens in Europe just as, if you are American, you think America is where it all happens. Well, it does not, of course. Some things — some of the worst things, some of the good things — do happen in America and Europe, but much that is of value to humanity is actually becoming more and more evident at a higher and higher level in some countries in South America, in China, in Russia. There is affirmation in all these fields for change, not the old style Communistic revolutionary leader but a new type of left-wing, committed-to-the-people democratic leader coming to the fore in several states in South America and elsewhere. That is a healthier way to go than the old, now dying, oligarchy of the Soviet groupings, both east and west. Democracy is a reality and is the preferred mode of social life by the Masters.

They do not work exactly as a democracy. Hierarchy, as the name suggests, is a hierarchy. They quite openly accept that, for example, Maitreya knows more than the Masters because He is more evolved, older, and has an awareness of aspects of cosmos which His immediate disciples do not have, even if They are sixth-degree initiates. It is a hierarchy, and They take it for granted that anyone more evolved will have a wider and more profound area of knowledge and wisdom, by the very nature of consciousness. However, They do work democratically in so far as each Master takes on a certain body of work and from His own consciousness makes that effective in the world. He is responsible for His own section of the work or teachings and has the democratic right to put forward His views at the collective Hierarchical meetings where all ideas are discussed and appraised.

We find it difficult to accept a hierarchical view of life, to accept differences in people. Countries like Holland, Sweden and Norway, for example, which are very democratic, find really distasteful the idea that there is a Hierarchy, that there are people Who are Masters. They always think that the Masters tell us what to do. As I have been at pains to say over the years, the Masters are not here to tell us what to do at all. The Masters will only advise and teach in the sense of revealing the results of actions. If we do this action, so and so will inevitably result, and if we do that action, then something quite different, probably preferable, will result. Then They leave the choice to us. If we are intelligent we take Their advice. They illuminate the results of the various actions which we can take. That is an extraordinary bonus to decision making — if you have a Master, a Teacher, a Guide Who tells you that if you do this then such and such will come out of it, or if you do that then another thing entirely will come out of it, then you can see which way you want to go. It is what you want; you have free will. I cannot over-emphasize that fact.

We really do not understand what free will is. We have an understanding of it in rather a superficial way, but we really do not understand how profound a quality free will is and why it is so impossible for the Masters to infringe our free will. Free will is the very element of our nature which makes evolution possible. Without free will we would not evolve. The Masters are in charge of the Plan of evolution so They are involved with evolution, and human evolution is part of it. If They were to infringe our free will, which is fundamental to being able to evolve at all, They would put a stop to Their own actions and put a stop to all evolution of humanity — so it will never happen. We must become aware of how important that free will is and not see it as something we hold on to even when we know we are doing the wrong thing.

Someone comes along, a teacher for example, somebody

who knows the answers and has been over the same ground and so knows that if you do this, then that will happen, and tells you so. If you take it as some infringement of your precious free will, then you are not going to benefit from that quality.

I know people who will not take the fact of the Masters' presence in the world even when They are acting openly. They will not take Hierarchical guidance because they are democrats and they will not take any kind of hierarchical supervision if they feel it as supervision over their right to be themselves and their right to be democratic. It is an obsession with democracy. They have brought democracy, rightly, to a very high level of importance in our social life and then they have deified it. They have made it an ideology which puts a barrier around themselves, so they cannot grow. They cannot accept anything higher than their democracy.

They are only men and woman and they are limited, as all men and women are, by their point in evolution. I do not know what the average point in evolution is of the governing, intelligent, politicians in the world. I would say it is something like 1.4 or 1.35. It is not enough. They are functioning astrally; they are not mentally polarized. They cannot make decisions objectively and so they make a mess of the world.

The people whom Maitreya and the Masters have been training, you will find, will be 1.5 or higher, probably even a few second-degree initiates, working from a higher level. They can see more objectively. They might still be fanatics and might still be sunk in their own particular ideology, but they will have a greater sense of the whole. They will have greater tolerance in the things that matter even if they are Christian fanatics or Muslim fanatics or whatever.

NATIONS — THE PEOPLE AND THEIR LEADERS

Q. I find it interesting that a country like Germany could in less than a half century go from having an evil leader, Hitler, to electing a leader like Willy Brandt, the man who led the panel that created a true consensus for the development of a model economic package for the future. Is this an example of how far humanity can go from one extreme to another in a positive direction?

A. It is certainly an example. I do not know that you could make it the example that is suggested here. It is extraordinary that there was Hitler and not so very long afterwards in Germany there was Willy Brandt. Brandt was elected. Hitler was not properly elected — it was manipulated. He was not elected by the people. Also, Willy Brandt was a third-degree initiate and was asked by Maitreya to create the Brandt Report. Willy Brandt was elected leader in a democratic process; he was a Democrat. He retired when he did not need to retire, because of some less than totally open action on the part of a subordinate. He took the blame. It was a great loss to Europe, a real loss to the world.

He was contacted by Maitreya very shortly after He came into the world. Maitreya came into London in July 1977 and in November 1977 He contacted Willy Brandt. He suggested that Brandt bring together a panel of economists from a whole spectrum of viewpoints, from extreme left to extreme right, from eminent men and women in as many countries as he could find. He brought together this panel, and by consensus they arrived at what was published as the Brandt Commission Report. It recommended nothing less than the sharing of resources and the reconstruction of our economic system — a tremendous achievement. It is a great loss to the world that Willy Brandt did not stay in power in Germany.

What is interesting is that Hitler dominated Germany from 1933 until the end of the war, 1945. He dominated because of the power of the two alternating members of the Black Lodge (what we know as the source of evil) who literally took over his body and obsessed him during that time. That evil was not Germany's evil, although obviously in another country it might not have happened. It did not happen in France, or Britain, or Holland. It did happen initially in Italy with Mussolini. That is why the Axis powers came together. Hitler, Mussolini and the group of militarists in Japan created a three-pointed force, a triangle. The energy poured through that triangle, which was potentized by the dark forces. The Masters in the Black Lodge know this science just as well as the Masters in the White Lodge, our Spiritual Hierarchy. They just use it for different purposes.

Germany as a nation is very young and, being young, its people are highly astral in their response to life, as are the US and many other countries. Had Germany been an older nation, Hitler probably would never have been allowed to rise. I am not saying it would not have been, but it might well not have been. The immaturity of a nation gives the opportunity for such men to emerge and take over. Where you have longer established systems, with their checks and balances, you tend not to get the same situation.

I do not think there is a corollary between Hitler and Willy Brandt as suggested in this question, because it is really to do with the readiness of the country and the emergence of the figures. If a country is ready to do something, the figures emerge to do it. An occult fact is that in every period of history souls come into incarnation with the ability to deal with the problems of the time. People come in, trained and ready, to answer the problems, and to bring humanity steadily forward.

From the Masters' point of view, the development of humanity is pretty steady. We see it as going up and down. For the Masters, the wars from 1914 to 1945 are one major war that allowed the Masters to come in. Maitreya announced His coming in 1945 because of the defeat of the forces of evil, the Lords of Materiality, as the Masters call them. The defeat of the Lords of Materiality made it possible for the Hierarchy to resume Their work on the physical plane ahead of schedule.

Q. How did Maitreya appear to Willy Brandt? Was he aware Who He was?
A. Yes, he knew Who it was, and he did the work. He was a third-degree initiate and knew what was happening.

Q. Is there always a combination of leaders and the people of that country that determine whether they act or do not act in regard to a problem? Would there ever be a time when there were potential leaders but they did not have the character or quality of the people necessary to carry out their ideas, or vice versa — people but no leaders?
A. It is not quite like that, but you often have leaders and not the support underneath for a democratic government. You get leaders, but the country is young and not politically mature and aware enough. So the leaders become dictators like Napoleon, who transformed Europe and created states that did not exist before.

The American 'Myth' of Freedom

Q. You have said that the world is waiting for the soul of America to manifest. Is this manifestation to come exclusively through the initiates in America or from the masses in the near future?
A. It comes through the initiates. The soul of a country always demonstrates through the initiates of that country. From the masses comes the personality expression. The personality expression of America is the 6th ray of Abstract Idealism or Devotion. Americans are indeed devoted to their own ideals. The ideal of freedom is probably the biggest ideal, at least the one that we hear of most. You do not hear about justice very much

because the idea of justice does not colour the consciousness of the masses of America.

America has elevated the concept of freedom to a degree which, to my mind, takes it beyond freedom. It is freedom to do what you like, under any conditions, with no restrictions. If you scratch an ordinary American, you see this powerful 6th ray, ready to brush aside all hindrances to get his own way. To the person, it is not a wrong way, but his own ideal way, and that is freedom.

The US President said that US freedom was being threatened by a little state called Iraq. It had no weapons of mass destruction. How could Iraq threaten America? The whole thing is absurd. I cannot understand how so many Americans fall for their government's claim that somehow or other, given that Iraq has no weapons of mass destruction, it was a threat to America. It was never a threat to America. It could be a threat to Kuwait, a threat to the Kurds certainly, a threat to Iran, perhaps, all over again, although I doubt it. Iraq could be a threat to Syria if it wanted to be. Syria is probably the only country that Iraq would really be a threat to, and it borders Iraq so it would be very easy. Syria has no weapons of mass destruction to speak of. Believing that Iraq was a threat to America is believing in a nonsense. For Mr Blair to persuade the British people and about one-third of his own party that Britain was threatened by Iraq is again a complete, utter nonsense. It is just not true.

Freedom has been elevated to a position where it is no longer freedom that you are talking about. Freedom is one of the imperative human needs. Without freedom, there is no real life. It is a great divine quality, but there is also justice. There cannot be freedom without justice, or justice without freedom.

The American 'myth' of freedom is based on the fact that the masses of Americans believe in what they call freedom, but obviously do not believe in justice. I have found that in the American mind they equate justice with the legal system. You are very concerned about legality. The legal system is very developed in America. But it has nothing to do with justice except legal justice. Justice is something else. Justice is to do with right relationship, just as freedom is to do with right relationship. You cannot have one without the other.

The masses of people making up the personality of America contrive somehow to see freedom as the overriding necessity for all peoples, and justice to be so far behind as to almost not be there. You have 275 million people in this country of whom some 44 million do not have any healthcare. This is unbelievable. That is a huge proportion of the population who cannot afford to go to the doctor, who cannot afford false teeth or dentistry if they need it, who are afraid to get ill because they have to take time off work and are not going to be paid for it. It is an abomination.

That is why, among Maitreya's priorities, He has stated: enough food, shelter, healthcare and education. These are the essentials for all peoples as a matter of course, as a human right. That is also in the United Nations Charter, which was largely written by President F.D. Roosevelt. You know about this and yet there is no emphasis in American thought on the concept of justice. They know what equality means, and they do not like it. They call it communism, socialism.

Maitreya says that no nation can work on one wheel. If you see a nation as a cart, it must have two wheels; otherwise it will not go. If one wheel alone is capitalism, it will not move. If one wheel alone is socialism, it will not move. The only thing that will make the cart, that is your political/economic structure, work properly is to have the best of socialism and the best of capitalism. The Masters advise 70 per cent socialism to 30 per cent capitalism as the best proportion.

Q. Why do we not hear anybody talk about the cause of terrorism?

A. Because they do not understand and are just afraid. I am not surprised, because it is quite a sophisticated view to see that there is a cause even behind terrorism. People are so frightened of terrorism, especially in the States, and especially since the 9/11 attack on the World Trade Center. The Americans are psychologically shocked to the core. It has transformed the thinking and feeling in America more than any other action since the World War. It is as if something terrible, absolutely unbearable, an affront to their ascendancy, to their invincibility, had happened, instead of saying, that was a terrorist attack and we must build up our defences against terrorism and move onto the next thing, whatever that happens to be. Not vengeance on the people of Afghanistan, who were not, on the whole, terrorists, and not against the people of Iraq, who were not terrorists and who have not invaded anyone for a decade (then it was against their neighbours and not America).

It is a very difficult concept for people to grasp, that there is a cause of terrorism. It is to do with the fact of the injustice which prevails in the world. That is a very difficult concept for Americans above all, and even for people of other nations, to take on board — the concept that justice is as real and important as freedom.

Q. How many third-degree and fourth-degree initiates are there in the USA?

A. I am not going to answer that, even though I could get the answer. This is another emphasis on the USA. You have to learn to forget somewhat about the USA. You see the USA as an extension of yourselves. The world is the real extension of ourselves.

We live in a world in which there are about 865,000 first-degree initiates, about 250,000 second-degree initiates, between 2,000 and 3,000 third-degree initiates, 450 fourth-degree initiates, and 63 Masters.

KARMA — THE LAW OF CAUSE AND EFFECT

Q. You said a number of former Nazis have incarnated in Israel. It seems they are continuing the same pattern from their previous life — oppression and racially-motivated abuse of others, taking land for the 'chosen' group. How does the Law of Karma help individual souls learn and evolve in this way?
A. The Law of Karma does not help individual souls to learn and evolve in that way. Certainly, the Law of Karma is at work in the displacement of these Nazi military and other leaders, who are acting in Israel as they would have done in Germany in their previous incarnation.

It is because of their ray make-up and because they find themselves in a similar situation. They see themselves as Israeli. They would simply read the problems of the time. The problems to them are that Israel is visited every other week by young men and women who blow themselves up when they get on a bus or enter a café, and kill Israelis. The Israelis hate this. They hate the unexpectedness of it; that is one of the terrors of terrorism.

How does the Law of Karma help individual souls learn and evolve in this way? That is seeing things from an idealistic point of view. The Law of Karma is not involved with idealism. The Law of Karma is a very benign law, which you yourself set in motion and which brings to you the events that you have initiated. As you think, you create thoughtforms. Your actions create causes. These causes make effects. The effects are what you experience. They make your life, for good or ill. That is the Law of Karma, and shows the need for harmlessness in every situation. That is what people do not know.

"Does the Law of Karma help individual souls learn and evolve in this way?" These people incarnated in Israel in relation probably to thousands of Jews in Germany that they had murdered, oppressed in every way. They grew to hate Jews for whatever reason. It was Hitler's aim to get rid of all the Jews in the world if he could do it. He could not do it, but the Nazis got rid of about 6 million in Europe. They are responsible, and have now come back as Jews.

It is not learning to evolve. It is the Law of Cause and Effect, that is, karma. They are living as the very people that they were so hateful to and oppressed in their previous incarnation. They are also bringing with them the quality of their ray structure, the energies which they use, which gave them power in Germany. These people were not the top people, but the people under them in the SS and army. It is not just the odd individual, there are a lot. Large numbers of Nazis have also reincarnated in Argentina and other places, including the USA.

Q. Can you say something about the correlation between the unleashing of the Forces of Materiality and the karmic repercussions of the people that they work through? Is the energy of the Antichrist and the energy of the Forces of Materiality one and the same?

A. Yes, they are one and the same. Hitler is no longer in incarnation; he is in what Christians would call purgatory. How long he will be there I have no idea, but a long time. There is a direct correlation with the evil effect that a person has through working with the forces of involution. The greater the impact of that in the world, the greater will be the karma of that person.

There are some people who are not essentially evil, like Stalin. Stalin, who was a second-degree initiate, was not evil. He was sort of 'grey', not 'black'. He was not essentially working with the same kind of energy. He was working for an ideal, for what he thought was for the benefit of Russia.

All the misdeeds that he carried out against individuals and millions of people, he did for the 'better' cause, the cause of his idea of the new Russia. It has an idealism that you can separate from the plain, simple evil of the forces working through Hitler and company. I do not include Stalin in that group, but he is grey. It is a personal misuse of power, and a lack of recognition of the difference between good and evil. Whereas Hitler (also a second-degree initiate), was literally obsessed by the forces, as to a lesser extent was Mussolini in Italy. But the correlation must always be with the amount of energy expended.

A second-degree initiate might touch the 'dark side' in an experimental way, looking for 'kicks', for something interesting, out of curiosity, knowing that it is not the thing to do, but nevertheless being tempted by it. A second-degree initiate is quite high, but not yet perfect. Not that a third-degree initiate is perfect, but a second-degree initiate is not Christed, not completely on the side of the Light. He could be either, and he can be used by either.

That is the problem for some second-degree initiates. They do not know where they stand. They do not know quite which they want. Stalin wanted power. He wanted a good life for the Russian people, but he was obsessed by his own ability to provide it. He could not provide it, without making many wrong decisions, but his aims were not evil. That is the difference.

It is to do with purpose. What was the purpose behind the action? If the purpose is evil, then the action is evil. If the purpose is good but the result is evil, there is probably less energy being expended and utilized in the process, so the karmic result would be less.

Q. Do we experience lives in which we receive the results of our previous action?
A. Of course. Your previous actions make your existing lives. That is exactly what karma does. The way our lives are led

now is the result of the actions we have made in the past and make today. It is not only the past. Karma is a dynamic law that pertains to every action we make. We do not stop making actions just because we are reborn. We start all over again, and do it very assiduously. If they are good actions, they bring about good karma. If they are destructive actions, they bring about pain and suffering.

Will these people suffer? The suffering that they caused, they will suffer. The suffering that someone else suffered as a result of their action, they will suffer in one way or another. It is not a mechanical law, but it is an exact law. It is as if the Lords of Karma weigh the quality of the energy expended from thought or action, and it comes back to you in like manner. Many of the people who are murdered in the world are working through a karmic situation.

Q. New karma is being made all the time, right? We cannot just assume that this person killed the other person in another life.
A. You cannot assume it, no.

Q. How do you know what is really going on then? You cannot know. You cannot assume that the karma is always only what is happening in this life. Somebody could just be doing something to you or somebody else for the first time.
A. Precisely. It is a dynamic process. You are dealing with a dynamic situation. There is old karma and new karma sitting side by side in everyone's consciousness. Of course, there is a first time for everything.

Q. So how will it end?
A. There is not an end. There has to be a resolution of the karma. For instance, I know a woman who in her present life was abused sexually by her father, which went on until she

was 14 or 15. That was a direct result of the fact that in the previous life she was the father and the father was the daughter, who was sexually abused by (now) the daughter. That was the result of a still earlier life in which the father was the father and the daughter was the daughter. It was successive exchanging relationships these three times. I asked the question you just asked, and my Master said: "It will be resolved in this life. It is unlikely to go beyond this life." That is karma.

Q. Can it be resolved through forgiveness?
A. Forgiveness is one of the major laws that mitigate and lessen the force of karma. Karma is a Law and it acts impersonally. There are four great Lords of Karma Who manipulate that Law. It is an impersonal Law, but if forgiveness is present in the person who has been harmed, that can mitigate tremendously the result of the Law. Maybe not totally, but it depends on the totality of the forgiveness. We are not all Jesus.

Q. What about the person forgiving themselves?
A. That is a different thing. Forgiving yourself has nothing to do with karma. It is guilt.

One of the major tasks of Maitreya is to remove guilt from humanity. People are guilty for no reason at all. They are guilty because they are too serious, or because they take on other people's problems, other people's hate, other people's lack of love, or whatever it happens to be. People feel guilty, especially children. Children whose families break up, their father and mother divorce, often feel personally to blame for the break-up of their parents, so traumatic is it for them. They think they did not love their parents enough, or they were not 'good', or they did 'wrong things'. It is absolutely nothing to do with the child at all, of course. It is the sensitivity of a child not to blame their father or mother but to blame themselves for the fact that the father and mother no longer live together.

That is related to self-forgiveness. People will not forgive themselves because they attach themselves to the result of their actions. You cannot alter the past. The past is the past. What you can alter is your attachment to the past. Where your attachment is fixed on your action or non-action in relation to a dead person, for instance — you did not look after them enough, or were not kind to them, or whatever — then you feel guilty. They die and you feel guilty that you were not nicer and more kind. There is nothing you can do about it. Perhaps it was not even true, but that is the feeling you have because they have died. You can no longer say to them what you might easily have said that would have made their life feel better.

If you attach yourself to that, you attach yourself to the guilt. You can go on blaming yourself for years, for not doing what you feel you might have done for this person. That is attachment, a negative thing. The attachment is holding back some part of your energy and attention. Your psyche is fixed there where it should be free. You are no longer free if you are attached even to something where you feel, "But I should have done …" Maybe you should have, but you cannot change it now that the situation is changed. You have to learn to give up the past, let it be, move on. Do not hold on and attach yourself to something that you cannot redress. It is gone.

Q. Is it true that possibly this sense of attachment is because we shall be held accountable karmically for these things?
A. It may be if you know the Law of Karma. That might well be the case. But usually I do not think it is, except if you believe God is looking down all the time, wagging His finger. You learned early on when you were 'bad', when you were not nice, when you were unkind, that God was watching. The whole world is brought up with this fantasy. God has too much to do to watch children tell lies!

RELIGIOUS PROBLEMS

Q. The Master Djwhal Khul said behind each problem in the world there was a religious problem. How will this problem be resolved — He said that it would take a long time?

A. That is a fact. It will take a long time. It is true that behind almost all the wars and fighting going on in the world is a religious division. There should not be any problem in a religious division. There have been places where Christians, Jews, Muslims have lived together in peace for hundreds of years. Spain was one of them. The religious division may be there, but as soon as there is an outer problem, for example, on the political/economic level, then the religious division comes to the fore and takes precedence. It is dealing with people's religious beliefs which, for many, are the strongest emotional ties they have.

When India was divided there were extraordinary massacres. Whole trainloads of Indians (Hindus) would be massacred by Muslims, while Pakistan was only being formed. They came from India and they were used to being Indians but they were not Hindus, they were Muslims. So there was conflict between Muslims and Hindus rather than between India and Pakistan. Then Bengal, which was part of Pakistan, became involved and, again, there was conflict between Muslims and Hindus. Then Bangladesh was formed and the same thing happened.

Whenever the outer political/economic pressures cannot be resolved relatively easily, it always turns into a religious divide. And it will go on. It was and still is so in Northern Ireland, although the fighting has stopped; it is so in Nigeria and other parts of Africa. It will be the last of all the big intolerances in the world to be resolved. The religious beliefs of a people are closer to them than anything else, which is another way of saying that the relationship of humanity to what we call God is stronger than we admit it to be. It is the strongest thought in the minds of most people in the world. Only the sophisticated intellectuals of Europe and a few other countries take a broader view and are not committed to any particular religion. Only if you have given up religion early in your life do you take this stance. Otherwise the fear of being separated from the country which you identify with your religion is paramount. Until we learn to be more tolerant, this will continue.

There are three big associations of mankind: political, economic and religious, which if wrongly handled become a corrupt ideology or totalitarianism. There are the political ideologues: Democrats, Fascists and Communists and so on. Political totalitarianism has waned and is really in decline. Economic totalitarianism at the moment is rampant. That is what Maitreya will be addressing more than anything else because it is the key to the others, to the tolerance which is needed to deal with the others. Last to go, but now at the height of its power and influence, is religious totalitarianism. If you are at the top there is only one way you can go, and that is down. Gradually its influence will lessen, but it will take time.

PRESENTING THE INFORMATION TO THE WORLD

Q. Can you give us any general advice about talking to the public?
A. People wonder how you should do this — how can you talk in such a way as to grasp their attention and move them, talking from the heart, making them understand what it is you are saying about the gaps between the developed world and the under-developed world. I think the key to it, although you may not like to hear this, is to do a lot of it, talk a lot. There is no way, if you are talking once a year, that you can get much practice in talking. You cannot practise your different qualities. You cannot bring them into active functioning because you do not give them the opportunity. If you talk, you have to

talk on a regular basis. I do not mean every day, but every other day will do! The more you do it the better you become at it.

Q. Who Maitreya is as the Lord of Love and Compassion was more deeply revealed to me in your lecture. Should we as a group focus our efforts in a more heart-centred manner in the work?

A. Yes, of course. But it is not like you choose: "Today I am going to be heart-centred. Yesterday I was very brain-centred, and I gave a wonderful lecture. Today I am giving a heart-centred lecture. It will reach different people. I will be more effective in a certain sphere, less effective to the brainy ones, but the hearty ones..." When you are lecturing, you use everything that you have. It is heart and head. It is not more heart-centred. Anybody giving this message has to be heart-centred. You cannot do it any other way. That does not mean to say you have no 'noddle' [brain]. You put it into words that people can understand, that affect them, that make them think. You use everything that is available in you to do it. You do not say: "I am such a heart person. I can only speak from the heart and everything I do comes from the heart." It is not like that. You just speak and your heart is involved; otherwise you would not be in this work. Your brain and mind are involved; otherwise you would not be giving the talk. When you are giving the talk, all of you is involved.

If you are doing it from a high enough concentration level you will find your intuition will work. The intuition is the voice of the soul. It is your soul taking over, using the equipment of your brain for the structuring of the ideas.

The ideas and the thoughts which really count with an audience allow you to rise above the ultimate boredom of saying the same thing over and over again, because that is what we are doing. I have been saying the same thing for 30 years, yet people think that every time they hear it, it is different. You say it as you feel it. You say it with your intuition. If you use your intuitive faculty, you will find you are saying things you know to be true but you have never thought or said before. But you know as soon as you have said that it is true. That is because your intuition is functioning, and you can only let it function when you are both relaxed and focused, focused high in the head.

Q. How can we translate our information into terms that people can relate to? How can we make it more real and more accessible for them?
A. Personal appearances, talks on radio and television, these are the weapons, the modus operandi of contacting the world and telling a story. As I have said, the more you do it, the better you will be at it. And the more you do it, the more you enjoy it.

If you are interested, you will make it interesting. If you are interested in the subject and the ideas and make them your own, tell them as if they were your own and relate them to the world, relate them to reality, and not as some dehydrated stuff, then inevitably your audience will respond. But you have to do it, and enjoy it. You have to forget about yourself and forget that it is you that is doing it and just do it. Learn to do it; that means do it often.

This is the greatest story in the world. It is never soon enough to talk about important things like the Reappearance of the Christ, for the first time in His own full, physical presence in the world, not an overshadowing of a disciple. This has never happened before and will never happen again. It is the culmination of 98,000 years of experience and living behind the scenes, as the Masters have done all this time. This is a time without precedent in the whole history of the world.

We have got the greatest story that has ever been given to

any group to talk about. It is priceless, wonderful. It has so many ramifications and is so close to the needs of humanity. You can put together the different facts that make it the most fascinating story. Journalists love it.

People love being entertained. Do not be afraid to make a joke if you can think of a joke. Better still just let the joke come. If it comes, snatch it, put it in.

Q. Could you explain why detachment is so important in presenting the information?
A. I would say that the question of detachment is central both to understanding the role of the groups in presenting this information to the world, and in working at the limit of one's capacities, inwardly and outwardly, learning to be detached without being isolated. This is the key, I think, to the statement I made about an insight into the heart of Maitreya, laden with all the anguish, the pain and suffering, misery, disappointment, yearning, of billions of people, and at the same time able to be funny, to be joyful in the extreme, spontaneous in His relations with people He meets in the street.

In an experience in one of the recent *Share International* magazines, for instance, a woman found she was being asked for the third time for 65 American cents. She began to get slightly annoyed because the first time she gave it gladly, the second time she gave it perhaps with a little more resistance, and this time she said: "Why is it always 65 cents?" Sixty-five cents is so specific, but it does not relate to anything, perhaps a 65-cent stamp and that is about all. Maitreya said (it was Maitreya Who asked for the 65 cents): "It is a gift from God." She said: "Sixty-five cents is a gift from God?" He said: "It is actually 70 cents." She was so amused by the quick response that she handed over, she did not say how much, but at least 65 cents. Then she realized He was giving her the opportunity to give, to learn to give. A lot of American people, I find, are good at giving. They have enormous generosity, but an almost equal number of Americans, and this applies equally all over the developed world, generally, are both generous and rather stingy. Stingy is an English word meaning not liking to part with money, especially to a stranger who is asking you for 65 cents for the third time. He made her understand that it was a gift, the opportunity to give a gift, even if only 65 cents. From the spiritual point of view, it is a gift of yourself.

I think people do not sufficiently understand this quality that the Masters have in such abundance. It is a generosity of heart, of spirit. They understand that to give is God-like. If someone is in need, it is a God-like gesture to give. Maitreya seems always to be returning to this, coming back as a beggar over and over again, asking for 65 cents or $2.

I met Him once when He asked for $2. He appeared as a well-dressed young man in Berkeley, California, who looked as if he did not particularly need $2. He said it was for gas, for his van. I looked up and down the street and saw no van. I did not mind at all giving him the $2, but I thought as I gave it, this can hardly be for your van. How much gas can you get for $2?

Q. What effect will Maitreya's emergence have on the Reappearance groups?
A. For one thing, it will be exhilarating. His coming out obviously will finish the work of making known the fact of Maitreya's presence in the world.

There is no doubt that a tremendous educational effort will be demanded of the groups because people everywhere will want to know. You will have to study if you have not already done so. Many of the questions, as is the case today, will be about Jesus, and about those around Jesus and His mother. People will want to know: "Did Jesus really marry Mary Magdalene? Did they have children? How many and what did they call them? Are any of them around now?" and so on. People are insatiable about such questions. You are going to have a lot of work to do, mainly educational. But there is also a world to save and the groups can get involved in that work.

Q. America is so diverse and big, we need to develop more active local participation. Would you please discuss the importance of local initiative and working as a group?
A. Local participation is the number one need. That is democracy. Politicians talk about democracy, but there really is not much democracy. They are the ones who make the decisions, and they are the government. In this way, your democracy is diminished.

Democracy is democracy not only through voting but through participation. The more participation there is, the more democracy is a reality. Until that pertains we can only say there is a move towards democracy, no real democracy in the world. If you want democracy, you have to participate. That means action. That does not mean leaving it to somebody else to participate — you have to do it. At a local level the more you do, the more effective you can become. If you participate as a group on a local level, your effect on a local level can be much more positive, actually more effective than it can be on the abstract level of national and international politics. It is very difficult for one person to change the actions of a government, but for one person to have a strong impact on a group at the local level is not impossible. This is happening all the time. People with something to say, with ideas that the community thinks are good and practical, are changing life in every country in the world. It is happening whether we are aware of it or not.

In every country, at local levels, a great change is happening; more and more people are making decisions about their own lives. They are doing this in the East, in countries that up till now never had any real representation, let alone participation. Here in the US you have representation but not very much participation, except in a very local sense. You want to make the best use of that. There are all sorts of groups who work in a participatory way in education, community life, sports, and so on.

Our subject is the Reappearance of the Christ, not sport or community work, although it might involve community work. If you work at community level, you might find many more supporters than you would think. You would be able to approach them one-to-one. There is nothing like one-to-one, face-to-face interaction in bringing the ideas of the Reappearance, and all that it means in terms of world transformation, to the consciousness of another person. They are more open when you are talking to them, and you are more persuasive when you do — provided you are persuasive without being invasive!

If you work with a group, you are more effective. Group work is the work of the future. The Aquarian energies can only be recognized, absorbed and used in group formation. You will find groups growing throughout the next hundreds of years. When you are a group, you potentize all the action that the individuals invest in the group. It is a very potent way to work.

It is no accident that whenever Hierarchy starts something, They create a group. They contact one person and give them a group, or give them the means of contacting a group, and then that group works together. That is why you get the Theosophical Society, the Arcane School, and our groups around the world who are working for the emergence of Maitreya and the Masters. Group work is the answer.

Q. Do you or the Masters have something specific you think would be best for us to do as outreach at this specific time?
A. Yes. More outreach. More of the same, or a bit better than the same. If you have been flagging, which you have been, maybe you have put up the wrong flags — too many Stars and

Stripes and not enough United Nations flags. You have to widen your horizons and stop thinking about yourselves, that is, America. Think of the world and the impact of America on the world at the present time. You have to broaden your concept of allegiance and give it to the world as a whole. In practical terms, that is the United Nations — not the Security Council, but the General Assembly, which is almost all the countries in the world.

Q. You mentioned that we are meant to be here, that our karma is to be in these groups. I was wondering whether this was for everyone or just for a few people?
A. There is a group involved in making the initial contact with the public about the information on the return of the Christ to the world. That group consists of between 4,000 and 5,000 people who have come into incarnation at this time, related karmically, not to the Reappearance of the Christ, of course, but to each other in relation to Hierarchy. They have been given the karmic opportunity (that is what it is, a karmic opportunity) to overcome the karma of their past: to do the work of preparing the way for the Christ, creating the climate of expectancy, so that He can enter our lives without infringing our free will; presenting not the Christ but the words, the ideas, the concerns of the Christ, to the world ahead of His open physical presence. In return, He gives to the groups His blessing and lights within them a fire which, as it gets hotter and hotter, drives them forward in evolution.

That is what is happening. Christ is giving them the opportunity to serve, an opportunity which is unbelievable. I probably do not know what the depth of the reality of that statement is, but I can tell you that this is an opportunity which is presented just now and will never be repeated because Hierarchy are returning to the world. Next time it will be a different story, a different situation. The Masters know the people who were offered this opportunity and they know that this one is sure, it is certain they are going to do it. They are going to work all they can. This one, well, they are going to do their best in a quiet way. And these, well, there is a question mark around whether they will do it or not, but if they have the commonsense to seize the opportunity, they will do it.

This is the whole point — the opportunity is presented but there is no infringement of free will. It is presenting the gift of service to the group. Somebody has to do it. They have a few more than 4,000 people, which does not sound very much in a global population of 6.5 billion, but they are all related to Hierarchy in some way. They are all disciples or aspirant to discipleship.

It is an opportunity presented to people who have something in common, a karmic relationship. They are members — at a low level, of course — of Hierarchy, and have been given an opportunity to serve in this plan of making the initial approach to humanity about the Reappearance 'story' and all the connected parts of it. It would never be done except for the exigencies of the time. It is part of the good luck (only it is not a matter of luck) of the people involved that they have done enough in their previous lives. Just call yourself lucky to hear about this story, lucky to have the opportunity to work with it, to make it your own and to be one of the gallant 4,000!

Q. Aren't there some other disciples who could be working as you do to make known the Christ's presence?
A. There were five people who you might have thought would be key people in the 4,000 people involved in this work around the world: one in New York, me in London, one in Geneva, one in Darjeeling, one in Tokyo, all chosen to be the first presenters. Around them would gather more, so that it would become a worldwide happening. This information would be coming from five major spiritual

centres across the world from New York to Tokyo, a brilliant plan, except that the one in New York does not believe. He has been to my lectures several times but does not believe the story. I am the one in London. The one in Geneva, like the one in New York, does not believe the story. They are both Christian mystics, influenced by people like Rudolf Steiner who died before the plan that it would be the Christ Himself was finalized. Steiner was adamant that the Christ could not return in a physical body and thought that when the Christ Principle awakened sufficiently in the hearts of men, then we could say the Christ is in the world. This is only one aspect of the Reappearance of the Christ. People who follow Steiner have closed their minds to the very possibility of the Reappearance of the Christ as a physical man in the world, quite apart from all the 40 or so Masters Who are likewise coming.

The man in Darjeeling is still asleep, and the one in Tokyo is a woman who believes *she* is Maitreya, so they are not doing a very good job. This was not the fault of Hierarchy, because They simply present the opportunity to serve. The disciples all have free will and have the right not to take up the work.

We have to make it happen. We have to 'make the noise' in the world that makes people understand that this is happening and so create the climate of hope, of expectancy for it to happen, and so raise the hope of humanity, who are desperate. They have to have hope for the future, and nothing so gives them hope as the thought of the Reappearance of the Christ or the Imam Mahdi or Maitreya Buddha or Krishna. It raises their spirits and alleviates their anxiety and tension.

Q. This is a question about diversity in presenting the Reappearance story. If it is true that four other senior disciples refused to present it to the public, then perhaps the story has so far been presented from one perspective only, that is, as a continuation of the Blavatsky/Bailey work. Would you like to comment, please?

A. True indeed, it has been, but I have never said these four others were senior disciples. I said there were four other disciples. I did not say any of them were senior. There is a difference. None of them were in touch with a Master. If they had been, they would probably have acted as I have. If I had not been in touch with a Master and received the information as they probably received it, I probably would not have acted either. But I had a Master saying: "Go on, get out and tell it to the world."

You have no idea how difficult it was. It was not my idea at all to go out and talk to the world. I would never have done it had I not been rather pushed to do it. So I do not blame those others for not coming forward. It is true, therefore, that it has largely come through as a continuation of the Blavatsky/Alice Bailey information, which I believe is the correct one. I could never have spoken in any other way. I am steeped in the Blavatsky and Alice Bailey teachings, which I believe are the direct teachings from Hierarchy. I am only interested in what I believe to be the truth.

Nevertheless, there are other ways in which this information could be presented. You could be a believing Christian. I am sure many people in the groups are believing Christians. They could go out and talk about this as the return of the Christ, and would not need to refer to Alice Bailey or Blavatsky or any of the teaching given. It could be presented in many different ways. I am not these other people, so I cannot present it in any other way than I do. But I am absolutely certain it can be presented in other ways.

For example, the Muslims await the Imam Mahdi. There were two Pakistani men who were sent to London about the time when Maitreya came there. They both had met a 'holy man', one in Lahore and the other in Karachi. They did not know each other, and the holy men were different, but each told them the same story. They were to go to London to prepare the way for the Imam Mahdi. One man was a journalist and involved in politics. He said: "No, I cannot. I have my work. I am a journalist and I am a member of the political party of Benazir Bhutto's father" (before he was killed). He said: "There is no way I can go." The holy man had told him months earlier that he would have to go to London, and had given him things he had lost years before and knew things about his family that only his family knew. He presented himself as somebody who was very knowledgeable. This holy man said: "If you do not go, events will conspire to force you to go."

The same thing happened with the other man, who was a lawyer. He said: "I cannot go. I have my law practice." The holy man said: "If you do not go, events will conspire to force you to go."

The upshot was that Mr Bhutto was killed and anybody connected with him became suspect. They were looking for members of Bhutto's party. I do not know what position the journalist held, but he was well-connected in the party. He had a brother living in the Asian community of London. He gave up his job and went to London, and got work as a journalist on a Pakistani paper.

The lawyer, meanwhile, found his business failing, and before it got too low he just sold it for the goodwill of his practice and he too went off to London. Those two men did not know each other, and did not meet until I put a full-page advertisement in one of the newspapers in the Asian community in London, saying that the Mahdi had returned to the world and was living in the Asian community in London. The information went around the community. These two men from Pakistan read it. It so happened that the brother of one of them knew the other one. So he invited the two together, and they found out that they had had exactly the same experience. Each in different cities, different holy men had given them the exact same instruction. So they decided to get in touch with me and I met them.

I had announced in May 1982 that Maitreya was in the Asian community of London, and that if well-known journalists of calibre went through the motions of looking for Him, He would come forward to them. I expected many foreign journalists to do this and asked these men to act as their guides into that rather closed Asian community, and they agreed.

However, the one who was a journalist just waited for Maitreya to tap him on the shoulder. The other read all he could about the Imam Mahdi, and in the process he turned himself into a fundamentalist Muslim. Since then he has written a book about the coming to the world of the Imam Mahdi.

You can present this information in the way of Christians, of Muslims, of Buddhists. Maitreya Buddha is awaited by all Buddhists. Japanese Buddhists think it is still about 5 billion 670 million years ahead, so there is no hurry. It can be presented as being about Krishna or Kalki Avatar, or as the Jewish Messiah. These all refer to Maitreya, whether knowingly or not.

I present it in the Hierarchical way, which I believe to be the most informed, the most true, the most profound, the least distorted. All the religious ways are distorted to some degree. It has taken hundreds or thousands of years for them to come down to us, and they all get distorted. Every holy scripture is discoloured to some degree. Only in the esoteric teaching, I believe, do you receive the true information.

If you are in touch with a Master, that is the best of all. You do not need any books or any other teaching. You can speak directly and that is the best. But that is rare; that is really rather rare.

Saving Ourselves

Q. At the New York City lecture, you said "We have to save ourselves", to great applause. This I found to be a great unifying expression within the context of the Reappearance, countering some concerns and/or projections about the World Teacher as a saviour.

A. There are two aspects to this question. One is the global, the other, personal. Maitreya comes to inspire humanity to save the planet, and humanity from destroying itself. It is through His teaching that He seeks to inspire us to make that change. This is the expectation that most people have of him as a 'Saviour'. But we have to do the work for ourselves. As He said long ago, every stone, every brick must be set in place by humanity itself: "I am the architect of the Plan, you are the willing builders of the Temple of Truth."

The second aspect concerns His relationship to each individual. In this case He is not a saviour but again a teacher. We must save ourselves by correct response to His teaching. No one else can do this, not even Maitreya Himself. The World Teacher is a saviour, but He does not come to save us. He comes to teach, and it is true we do the saving. By the correct response to the teachings, that is, making the teachings a dynamic force within our life, we save ourselves. Saving is knowing. When you become and are the Self, you are saved.

It has been presented to the world by the Christian groups for 2,000 years in terms of a Saviour coming to the world to save humanity from the results of their sins. But it has no relation to sin. It is about self-transformation. We change ourselves and enter the process of being saved. It is a stage-by-stage process.

We save ourselves in response to the teachings and above all the application of the teachings to oneself. You can hear teachings and they remain as teachings, as they have done for 2,000 years to millions of people. The teachings of Maitreya through Jesus, which people have heard and put into the Bible, have been either explained away or are still as relevant today as they were, but have not been applied.

If we do not apply the teachings, if they are not a dynamic force within us, and therefore a force for change, we do not become saved. Correctly applied, daily, weekly, yearly, the teachings transform us, bit by bit. We come closer to our soul, imbibe more of the soul's energy into ourselves, more of the light of the soul. We bring more subatomic matter into our bodies, so changing them, spiritualizing and gradually perfecting them. That is saving yourself — growing into the likeness of the soul.

The soul seeks to express itself through its vehicle, the man or woman, but they have to respond to the teachings. That is why the Teacher comes, to remind us once again of the Laws: the Law of Karma, the Law of Rebirth, the Law of Harmlessness. We have to apply these laws correctly, dynamically to our lives, not just as an idea that remains in the head but does not do anything. If it is only a memory in the brain, it does not do anything at all. We have to actually apply it and make it into a yeast so that it changes us. It lifts us and changes us. You have to change according to the teachings.

It is not knowledge per se. It is the instinctive response to the dynamic of the teaching. It is a process, not just words, not just homilies, not just something to remember. It does not matter if you remember it or not in terms of words. What does matter is if it becomes an active process in your life, and leads you from awareness to awareness, initiation to initiation, and eventually to perfection. That is being saved, and nobody can do it but oneself.

MAITREYA STEPS FORWARD

by the Master —, through Benjamin Creme

The emergence of Maitreya is all but accomplished. His open, public work will commence really very soon. From then will begin the process of teaching and becoming known, gradually, to the peoples of the world. The time that this will take remains unclear, but it should proceed relatively quickly. At first, of course, there may be much opposition to His views and the nature of His advice. This is only to be expected, so far from the prevailing thinking is His thought. Gradually, however, Maitreya's incisive mind will cut through and expose the flaws in present beliefs about the environment and on matters social, economic and political. The logic and wise understanding of His words will convince many to listen and contemplate further, while His Ray will penetrate the hearts of millions and turn His simple words into revelations of Truth. No one, as yet, knows the loving power of Maitreya, nor can men fathom His inscrutable wisdom.

As millions rally to His cause, demanding peace and justice through sharing and understanding, men will be swept up and galvanized by new hope and a longing for brotherhood and right relationship. They will demand change on a scale hitherto unknown. The governments and men of power will be forced to respond to the demands, and bit by bit, the edifice against change will crumble before the onslaught of a now empowered voice of public opinion. Thus, by logic, revelation and the trust engendered by His love, will Maitreya harness the goodwill which exists, even if unknown, in every heart.

Maitreya will speak to millions of men through television and radio. All will have the opportunity to share in His blessing which will accompany every appearance. Thus the people worldwide will become familiar with His message and the uplifting of their hearts. Much speculation will surround His identity and many will be the theories presented, but all in their different ways will see Him as the harbinger of the new, a conveyor of wholesome truths and as a way-shower of a lifestyle close to their hearts.

Of course, there will be those who feel threatened by His ideas, and who will attempt to stop His progress but, more and more, the beauty and good sense of His words will inspire the people of all the nations to see Him as their spokesman and leader. Thus will it be. The people will call for Him to speak on their behalf to the world at large, and the Day of Declaration will be announced.

This day, like none other before or after, will give Maitreya the opportunity to reveal His name, title and purpose, as the World Teacher for the New Age, the leader of the Spiritual Hierarchy and the Expected One of all religious groups. As the friend and teacher of all who need His help will He present Himself; as a simple man Who knows the pain and suffering of men and seeks to ease their lot, Who loves all totally, without condition, and Who has come to show us the steps to joy.

Such a one is about to step before the world and give His advice to all. We may have heard the words before. Now, with His blessing, we shall understand their meaning, and act.

(*Share International,* January/February, 2007)

THE 'HAND' OF MAITREYA

This photograph shows the handprint of Maitreya Himself, miraculously manifested on a bathroom mirror in Barcelona, Spain in 2001. It is not a simple handprint but a three-dimensional image with photographic detail.

By placing your hand over it, or simply looking at it, Maitreya's healing and help can be invoked (subject to Karmic Law). Until Maitreya emerges fully, and we see His face, it is the closest He can come to us.

"My help is yours to command, you have only to ask."
Maitreya, the World Teacher
from Message no. 49

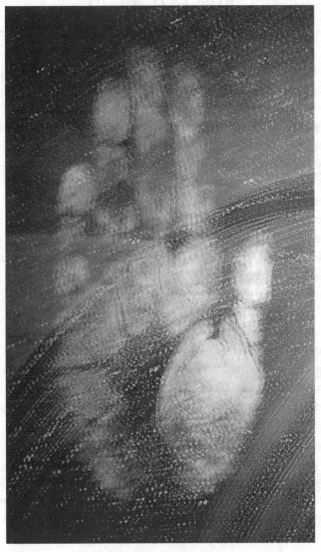

The Hand of Maitreya

THE GATHERING OF THE
FORCES OF LIGHT

by the Master —, through Benjamin Creme

Important events are taking place in many parts of the world. People everywhere will be astonished by the reports. These will include sightings, in unprecedented numbers, of spacecraft from our neighbouring planets, Mars and Venus in particular. Nothing like this increased activity, over vast areas of the Earth, will have been seen before. Those who have steadfastly refused to take seriously the reality of this phenomenon will find it difficult to deny. More and more accounts of contact with the occupants of the spacecraft will add their testimony to the fact of their existence. Miraculous happenings of all kinds will continue and multiply in number and variety. The minds of men will be baffled and amazed by these wonders, and this will cause them to ponder deeply.

Into this wonder-filled, wondering world Maitreya will quietly enter and begin His open work. He will be asked to counter their doubts and fears, to explain these happenings and He will vouchsafe their validity. These extraordinary events will continue unabated and cause many to prophesy the ending of the world. Maitreya, however, will continue in His simple way and interpret differently these events.

Thus will Maitreya encourage men to see the marvellous breadth and scope of life, the many layers of which man knows but little till now. Gently He will introduce them bit by bit to the basic truths of our existence, the Laws which govern it, and the benefits achieved by living within these Laws. He will acquaint man with the vastness of our Galaxy and show that, in time, men of Earth will conquer Space and Time. He will encourage men to seek within, as well as without, for the answers to their problems, and validate their constant connection to each other and to Cosmos. He will remind human-ity of its long history and of the many perils which man has overcome. He will sow the seeds of faith in our own illustri-ous future and vouchsafe the eternal divinity of man. He will show that the path of life, the evolutionary journey, leads un-failingly upwards as well as for ever onwards, and that to make the journey together, as brothers and sisters, is the surest way and the way most lit by joy. Look, then, for the signs of Maitreya's entrance, make it known, and uplift the hope of your brothers.

(*Share International*, March 2007)

[Editor's note: As the Master so vividly illustrated in this ar-ticle, we may look forward to widespread sightings of space-craft and other signs of Maitreya's emergence. The reports of such sightings from all over the world are published in *Share International* magazine.]

CROP CIRCLES

The crop circles are created by what is generally called UFO activity. The UFOs come in the main from Mars and Venus, not from outside our solar system. All the planets of this system are populated, though if you went to Mars or Venus you would see no one at all — they are all in higher etheric matter. The UFO phenomenon is distinctly related to the Reappearance of the Christ and the externalization of the work of the Hierarchy, and we owe them a great debt. Their surveillance of this planet is total and energetically of enormous benefit to the world.

What the Space People are doing in the crop circles in particular is recreating to a certain degree the 'grid' of our Earth's magnetic field on the physical plane. Each of these crop circles is a chakra, as it were, a vortex of magnetic energy, and they are spreading out around the world, having started in England. They are all 'ideograms', and if you were familiar with the 'ideography' of ancient Atlantis you would recognize some of them. They are meant not to be recognized as to their meaning but they do have a meaning, and many people will 'intuit' these. They are a reminder of the ancient connection with the Space Brothers.

(*Share International,* July/August 1991)

Straight Soley, Berkshire, UK, 20 July 2006. © Steve Alexander

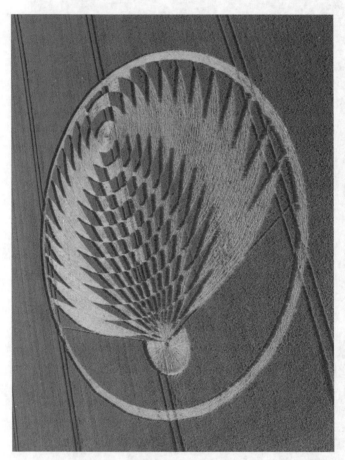

Uffington Castle, Oxfordshire, UK, 8 July 2006. © Steve Alexander

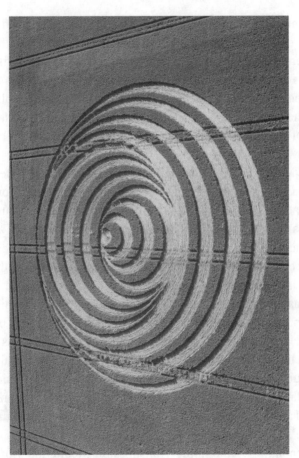

Aldbourne, Wiltshire, UK, 14 July 2006. © Steve Alexander

TRANSMISSION MEDITATION

A BRIEF EXPLANATION

A group meditation providing both a dynamic service to the world and powerful, personal spiritual development.

Transmission Meditation is a group meditation established to better distribute spiritual energies from their Custodians, the Masters of Wisdom, our planetary Spiritual Hierarchy. It is a means of 'stepping down' (transforming) these energies so that they become accessible and useful to the general public. It is the creation, in co-operation with the Hierarchy of Masters, of a vortex or pool of higher energy for the benefit of humanity.

In March 1974, under the direction of his Master, Benjamin Creme formed the first Transmission Meditation group in London. Today there are hundreds of such groups around the world, and new groups are forming all the time.

Transmission Meditation groups provide a link whereby Hierarchy can respond to world need. The prime motive of this work is service, but it also constitutes a powerful mode of personal growth. Many people are searching for ways in which to improve the world; this desire to serve can be strong, but difficult, in our busy lives, to fulfil. Our soul needs a means to serve, but we do not always respond to its call, and so produce disequilibrium and conflict within ourselves. Transmission Meditation provides a unique opportunity for service in a potent and fully scientific way with the minimum expenditure of one's time and energy.

Benjamin Creme holds Transmission Meditation workshops around the world. During the meditation he is overshadowed by Maitreya, the World Teacher, which allows Maitreya to confer great spiritual nourishment on the participants. Many people are inspired to begin Transmission Meditation after attending such a workshop, and many acknowledge having received healing in the process.

[Please refer to *Transmission: A Meditation for the New Age* by Benjamin Creme, Share International Foundation]

THE GREAT INVOCATION

From the point of Light within the Mind of God
Let light stream forth into the minds of men.
Let Light descend on Earth.

From the point of Love within the Heart of God
Let love stream forth into the hearts of men.
May Christ return to Earth.

From the centre where the Will of God is known
Let purpose guide the little wills of men —
The purpose which the Masters know and serve.

From the centre which we call the race of men
Let the Plan of Love and Light work out
And may it seal the door where evil dwells.

Let Light and Love and Power
restore the Plan on Earth.

●

The Great Invocation, used by the Christ for the first time in
June 1945, was released by Him to humanity to enable man
himself to invoke the energies which would change our world,
and make possible the return of the Christ and Hierarchy. This
is not the form of it used by the Christ. He uses an ancient formula, seven mystic phrases long, in an ancient sacerdotal
tongue. It has been translated (by Hierarchy) into terms which
we can use and understand, and, translated into many languages, is used today in every country in the world.

THE PRAYER FOR THE NEW AGE

I am the creator of the universe.

I am the father and mother of the universe.

Everything comes from me.

Everything shall return to me.

Mind, spirit and body are my temples,

For the Self to realize in them

My supreme Being and Becoming.

●

The Prayer for the New Age, given by Maitreya, the World Teacher, is a great mantram or affirmation with an invocative effect. It will be a powerful tool in the recognition by us that man and God are One, that there is no separation. The 'I' is the Divine Principle behind all creation. The Self emanates from, and is identical to, the Divine Principle.

The most effective way to use this mantram is to say or think the words with focused will, while holding the attention at the ajna centre between the eyebrows. When the mind grasps the meaning of the concepts, and simultaneously the will is brought to bear, those concepts will be activated and the mantram will work. If it is said seriously every day, there will grow inside you a realization of your true Self.

GLOSSARY OF ESOTERIC TERMS

Age — World cycle, approximately 2,500 years, determined by the relation of the Earth, Sun and constellations of the zodiac.

Ageless Wisdom — An ancient body of spiritual teaching underlying all the world's religions as well as all scientific, social and cultural achievements. First made available in writing to the general public in the late 1800s by Helena Petrovna Blavatsky and in this century by Alice A. Bailey, Helena Roerich and Benjamin Creme.

Ajna centre — The energy centre (chakra) between the eyebrows. Directing centre of the personality. Its correspondence on the physical level is the pituitary gland.

Antahkarana — An invisible channel of light forming the bridge between the physical brain and the soul, built through meditation and service.

Antichrist — Energy of the Will aspect of God, in its involutionary phase, which destroys the old forms and relationships, for example at the end of an age, to prepare the way for the building forces of the Christ Principle. Manifested in Roman times through the emperor Nero and in modern times through Hitler and six of his associates.

Aquarius — Astronomically, the age of Aquarius, now commencing and lasting 2,350-2,500 years. Esoterically, refers to the Water Carrier, the age of Maitreya, and to the spiritual energy of Aquarius: that of synthesis and brotherhood.

Ashram — A Master's group. In the Spiritual Hierarchy there are 49 ashrams, seven major and 42 subsidiary, each headed by a Master of Wisdom.

Astral body — The emotional vehicle of an individual.

Astral plane — The plane of the emotions, including the polar opposites such as hope and fear, sentimental love and hate, happiness and suffering. The plane of illusion.

Astral Polarization — The focus of consciousness is on the astral plane. The first race, the Lemurian, had the goal of perfecting physical-plane consciousness. Atlantean man's goal was the perfecting of astral/emotional consciousness. The majority of humanity today are still polarized on the astral plane. See also Mental Polarization.

Avatar — A spiritual Being Who 'descends' in answer to mankind's call and need. There are human, planetary and cosmic Avatars. The latter would be called 'Divine Incarnations'. Their teaching, correctly apprehended and gradually applied by humanity, expands our understanding and presents the next step forward in humanity's evolutionary development.

Avatar of Synthesis — A great cosmic Being Who embodies the energies of Will, Love, Intelligence and another energy for which we have as yet no name. Since the 1940s He has been sending these energies into the world, gradually transforming division into unity.

Buddha — Last Avatar of the age of Aries. Previous World Teacher Who manifested through the Prince Gautama around 500 BC. The Embodiment of Wisdom, He currently acts as the 'Divine Intermediary' between Shamballa and Hierarchy. Buddhists expect their next great teacher under the name Maitreya Buddha.

Buddhi — The universal soul or mind; higher reason; loving understanding; love-wisdom. The energy of love as the Masters experience it.

Buddhic plane — Plane of divine intuition.

Causal body — The vehicle of expression of the soul on the causal plane. The receptacle where consciousness of one's evolutionary point of development is stored.

Causal plane — The third of the four higher mental planes on which the soul dwells.

Chakras — Energy centres (vortices) in the etheric body related to the spine and the seven most important endocrine glands. Responsible for the co-ordination and vitalization of all the bodies (mental, astral and physical) and their correlation with the soul, the main centre of consciousness. There are seven major chakras and 42 lesser ones.

Christ — A term used to designate the head of the Spiritual Hierarchy; the World Teacher; the Master of all the Masters. The office presently held by the Lord Maitreya.

Christ Consciousness — The energy of the Cosmic Christ, also known as the Christ Principle. Embodied for us by the Christ, it is at present awakening in the hearts of millions of people all over the world. The energy of evolution per se.

Day of Declaration — The day on which Maitreya will make Himself known to the world during a worldwide radio and television broadcast. Even those who are not listening or watching will hear His words telepathically in their own language and, at the same time, hundreds of thousands of spontaneous healings will take place throughout the world. The beginning of Maitreya's open mission in the world.

Deva — Angel or celestial being belonging to a kingdom in nature evolving parallel to humanity, and ranging from subhuman elementals to superhuman beings on a level with a planetary Logos. They are the 'active builders', working intelligently with substance to create all the forms we see, including the mental, emotional and physical bodies of humanity.

Energy — From the esoteric point of view, there is nothing but energy in the whole of the manifested universe. Energy vibrates at various frequencies, and the particular frequency determines the form which the energy will take. Energy can be acted upon and directed by thought.

Esotericism — The philosophy of the evolutionary process both in man and the lower kingdoms in nature. The science of the accumulated wisdom of the ages. Presents a systematic and comprehensive account of the energetic structure of the universe and of man's place within it. Describes the forces and influences that lie behind the phenomenal world. Also, the process of becoming aware of and gradually mastering these forces.

Etheric Body — The energetic counterpart of the physical body, composed of seven major centres (chakras) and 42 minor centres, a network which connects all the centres, and infinitesimally small threads of energy (nadis) which underlie every part of the nervous system. Blockages in the etheric body can result in physical illnesses.

Etheric Planes — Four planes of matter finer than the gaseous-physical. As yet invisible to most people.

Evil — Anything which impedes evolutionary development.

Evolution — The process of spiritualization of matter; the way back to the Source. The casting aside of the veils of delusion and illusion leading eventually to cosmic consciousness.

Forces of Light (Forces of Evolution) — The Spiritual Hierarchy of our planet. Planetary centre of Love-Wisdom. See also Spiritual Hierarchy.

Forces of Darkness (Forces of Evil, Forces of Materiality) — The involutionary or materialistic forces which uphold the matter aspect of the planet. When they overstep their role and impinge upon the spiritual progress of humanity, they are

115

designated as 'evil'.

Glamour — Illusion on the astral plane. The condition when the mind becomes veiled by emotional impulses generated on astral levels, preventing the mind's eye from clearly distinguishing reality. Examples: fear, self-pity, criticism, suspicion, self-righteousness, over-materiality.

God (see also Logos) — The great Cosmic Being Who ensouls this planet, embodying all the Laws and all the energies governed by those Laws, which make up everything that we see and cannot see.

Great Invocation — An ancient formula, translated by Hierarchy for the use of mankind to invoke the energies which will change our world. Translated into many languages, it is used daily by millions of people.

Guru — A spiritual teacher.

Hierarchy — See Spiritual Hierarchy.

Hierophant — The Initiator. Either the Christ, at the first two planetary initiations, or the Lord of the World, at the third and higher initiations.

Illusion — Deception on the mental plane. The soul, using the glamoured mind as its instrument, obtains a distorted picture of the phenomenal world.

Imam Mahdi — The prophet Whose return is awaited by some Islamic sects in order that He can complete the work started by Mohammed.

Incarnation — Manifestation of the soul as a threefold personality, under the Law of Rebirth.

Initiation — A voluntary process whereby successive and graded stages of unification and at-onement take place between the man or woman in incarnation, his/her soul, and the divine Monad or 'spark of God'. Each stage confers on the initiate a deeper understanding of the meaning and purpose of God's Plan, a fuller awareness of his/her part in that Plan, and an increasing ability to work consciously and intelligently towards its fulfilment.

Involution — The process whereby spirit descends into matter, its polar opposite.

Jesus — A Master of Wisdom and disciple of the Christ, Maitreya. Allowed the Christ to work through Him during the period fromHis baptism to the crucifixion. In the coming time, He will play a major role in reinspiring and reorienting the whole field of Christian religion. As the Master Jesus, He works closely with Maitreya, often appearing to people (in disguise).

Karma — Eastern name for the Law of Cause and Effect. The basic Law governing our existence in this solar system. Every thought we have, every action we make, sets into motion a cause. These causes have their effects, which make our lives, for good or ill. Expressed in biblical terms: "As you sow, so shall you reap."; in scientific terms: "For every action there is an equal and opposite reaction."

Krishna — A great Avatar Who appeared around 3,000 BC and served as the vehicle of manifestation for the Lord Maitreya during the age of Aries. By demonstrating the need to control the astral/emotional nature, Krishna opened the door to the second initiation. Hindus expect a new incarnation of Krishna at the end of Kali Yuga, the dark age.

Law of Cause and Effect (Law of Action and Reaction) — See Karma.

Law of Rebirth — See Reincarnation.

Logos — God. The Cosmic Being Who ensouls a planet (Planetary Logos), a solar system (Solar Logos), a galaxy (Galactic Logos) and so on to infinity.

Lord of the World — See Sanat Kumara.

Maitreya — The World Teacher for the age of Aquarius. The Christ and head of the Spiritual Hierarchy of our planet. The Master of all the Masters.

Man/Woman — The physical manifestation of a spiritual Monad (or Self), which is a single spark of the One Spirit (God).

Manas — Higher mind.

Mantram — Formula or arrangement of words or syllables which, when correctly sounded, invokes energy.

Masters of Wisdom — Individuals Who have taken the fifth initiation, having passed through all the experiences that life in this world offers and, in the process, having acquired total mastery over themselves and the laws of nature. Custodians of the Plan of evolution and all the energies entering this planet which bring about the fulfilment of the Plan.

Meditation — Scientific means of contacting one's soul and of eventually becoming at one with the soul. Also the process of being open to spiritual impression and thus to co-operation with the Spiritual Hierarchy.

Mental body — The vehicle of the personality on the mental planes.

Mental plane — The plane of the mind where the mental processes take place.

Mental Polarization — The focus of consciousness on the mental plane. The shifting of consciousness on to the mental plane begins about half-way between the first and second planetary initiations.

Monad/Self — Pure Spirit reflecting the triplicity of Deity: (1) Divine Will or Power (the Father); (2) Love-Wisdom (the Son); (3) Active Intelligence (the Holy Spirit). The 'spark of

God' resident in every human being.

Occult — Hidden. The hidden science of energy (see Esotericism).

Overshadowing — A voluntary co-operative process in which a Master's consciousness temporarily enters and works through the physical, emotional and mental bodies of a disciple.

Permanent atoms — The three atoms of matter — physical, astral and mental — around which the bodies for a new incarnation are formed. They retain the vibratory rate of the individual at the moment of death, guaranteeing that the energetic evolutionary 'status' thus far achieved will be carried over into successive lives.

Personality — Threefold vehicle of the soul on the physical plane, consisting of a mental, an emotional (astral) and a physical-etheric body.

Physical plane — The lowest vibrational states of substance, including: dense-physical, liquid, gaseous and etheric matter.

Plane — A level of manifestation.

Planetary Logos — Divine Being ensouling a planet.

Pralaya — A non-mental, non-astral, non-material state of existence somewhere between death and rebirth, where the life impulse is in abeyance. An experience of perfect peace and unending bliss prior to taking the next incarnation. Corresponds to the Christian idea of paradise.

Rays — The seven streams of universal divine energy, each the expression of a great Life, Whose interaction at every conceivable frequency creates the solar systems, galaxies and universes. Movement of these energies, in spiralling cycles, draws all Being into and out of manifestation, colouring and saturating it with specific qualities and attributes.

Rays of Nations — Each nation is governed by two rays, a soul ray, which is sensed and expressed by the initiates and disciples of the nation; and a personality ray which is the dominant mass influence and expression. From time to time, through the activities of the initiates and disciples of a country, the soul ray may be given expression and the true quality of the nation can be seen.

Reincarnation (Law of Rebirth) — The process which allows God, through an agent (ourselves) to bring Itself down to Its polar opposite — matter — in order to bring that matter back into Itself, totally imbued with the nature of God. The Law of Karma draws us back into incarnation until gradually, through the evolutionary process, we reveal more truly our innate divinity.

Sanat Kumara — The Lord of the World; the etheric-physical expression of our Planetary Logos Who dwells on Shamballa. A great Being, originally from Venus, Who sacrificed Himself to become the personality vehicle for the ensouling deity of our planet 18.5 million years ago. The nearest aspect of God that we can know.

Self/Monad — The divine spark within every human being.

Self-realization — The process of recognizing and expressing our divine nature.

Shamballa — A centre of energy; the major centre in the planet. It is located above the Gobi Desert on the two highest etheric planes. From it and through it flows the Shamballa Force — the energy of Will or Purpose. It corresponds to the crown centre (chakra).

Solar Logos — Divine Being ensouling our solar system.

Soul (Ego, Higher Self, inner ruler, Christ within, Son of Mind, Solar Angel) — The linking principle between Spirit and matter; between God and His form. Provides consciousness, character and quality to all manifestation in form.

Spirit — As used by Maitreya, a term meaning the sum total of all the energies — the life force — animating and vitalizing an individual. Also used, more esoterically, to mean the Monad which reflects itself in the soul.

Spirit of Peace or Equilibrium — A cosmic Being Who assists the work of Maitreya by overshadowing Him with His energy. He works closely with the Law of Action and Reaction, to transform the present chaotic conditions into the opposite state in exact proportion.

Spiritual — The quality of any activity which drives the human being forward towards some form of development — physical, emotional, intuitional, social — in advance of his/her present state.

Spiritual Hierarchy (White Brotherhood, Society of Illumined Minds) — The Kingdom of God, the Spiritual Kingdom or the Kingdom of souls, made up of the Masters and initiates of all degrees and Whose purpose is to implement the Plan of God. Planetary centre of Love-Wisdom.

Transmission Meditation — A group meditation for the purpose of 'stepping down' (transforming) spiritual energies emanating from the Spiritual Hierarchy of Masters which thus become accessible and useful to the general public. It is the creation of a vortex or pool of higher energy for the benefit of humanity. This is a form of service which is simple to do, and is at the same time a powerful means of personal growth. There are hundreds of Transmission Meditation groups active in many countries around the world.

Triangle — A group of three people who link up each day in thought for a few minutes of creative meditation.

Vehicle — The form by means of which higher beings find

expression on the lower planes. The physical, astral and mental bodies, for instance, form the vehicles of the soul on lower levels.

Vibration — Movement of energy. All energy vibrates at its own particular frequency. The evolutionary process proceeds through a heightening of the vibrational rate in response to higher incoming energies.

World Teacher — The head of the Spiritual Hierarchy in any given cycle. The Master of all the Masters. The office held at present by the Lord Maitreya.

Yoga — Union of the lower nature with the higher. Also, different forms and techniques to gain control of the physical, astral or mental bodies.

BOOKS BY BENJAMIN CREME
(Listed in order of publication)

The Reappearance of the Christ and the Masters of Wisdom
In his first book, Benjamin Creme gives the background and pertinent information concerning the emergence of Maitreya (the Christ), as World Teacher for the New Age now dawning. Expected under different names by all religious groups, Maitreya comes to help us create co-operation among the many ideological factions, galvanize world goodwill and sharing, and inspire sweeping political, social, economic and environmental reforms. Benjamin Creme puts the most profound event of the last 2,000 years into its correct historical and esoteric context and describes what effect the World Teacher's presence will have on both the world's institutions and the average person. Through his telepathic contact with a Master of Wisdom, Creme offers insights on such subjects as the soul and reincarnation; fear of death; telepathy; meditation; nuclear energy; ancient civilizations; UFOs; problems of the developing world; a new economic order; the Antichrist; and the 'Last Judgement'.
1st edition 1979. 2nd edition 2007. ISBN: 978-90-71484-32-2, 288pp.

Messages from Maitreya the Christ
During the years of preparation for His emergence, Maitreya gave 140 Messages through Benjamin Creme during public lectures in London from 1977 to 1982. The method used was mental overshadowing and a telepathic rapport thus set up.

Maitreya's Messages of sharing, co-operation and unity inspire readers to spread the news of His reappearance and to work urgently for the rescue of millions suffering from poverty and starvation in a world of plenty. In Message No. 11 Maitreya says: "My Plan is to show you that the way out of your problems is to listen again to the true voice of God within your hearts, to share the produce of this most bountiful of worlds among your brothers and sisters everywhere. . . ."

Maitreya's words are a unique source of wisdom, hope and succour at this critical time of world change, and when read aloud these profound yet simple Messages invoke His energy and blessing.

1st edition Vol. I 1981, Vol. II 1986. 2nd, combined, edition 1992, reprinted 2001. ISBN 978-90-71484-22-3 ,286pp.

Transmission: A Meditation for the New Age

Transmission Meditation is a form of group meditation for the purpose of 'stepping down' (transforming) spiritual energies which thus become accessible and useful to the general public. It is the creation, in co-operation with the Hierarchy of Masters, of a vortex or pool of higher energy for the benefit of humanity.

Introduced in 1974 by Benjamin Creme, under the direction of his Master, this is a form of service which is simple to do and is at the same time a powerful means of personal growth. The meditation is a combination of two yogas: Karma Yoga (yoga of service) and Laya Yoga (yoga of energy or chakras). It is a service in which we can be involved for the rest of our lives knowing that we are helping the evolution of humanity into, and beyond, the New Age. There are hundreds of Transmission Meditation groups active in many countries around the world.

In this practical and inspiring book Benjamin Creme describes the aims, technique and results of Transmission Meditation, as well as the underlying purpose of the meditation for the development of disciples.

1st edition 1983. 5th edition 2006. ISBN 978-90-71484-35-3, 212 pp.

A Master Speaks

Humanity is guided from behind the scenes by a highly evolved and illumined group of men Who have preceded us along the path of evolution. These Masters of Wisdom, as They are called, seldom appear openly, but usually work through Their disciples – men and women who influence society through their work in science, education, art, religion, politics, and in every department of life.

British artist Benjamin Creme is a disciple of a Master with Whom he is in close telepathic contact. Since the launching of *Share International*, the magazine of which Benjamin Creme is editor, his Master has contributed to every issue an inspiring article on a wide range of subjects: reason and intuition; the new civilization; health and healing; the art of living; the need for synthesis; justice is divine; the Son of Man; human rights; the law of rebirth; the end of hunger; sharing for peace; the rise of people power; the brightest future; co-operation – and many more.

The major purpose of these articles is to draw attention to the needs of the present and the immediate future time, and to give information about the teachings of Maitreya, the Master of all the Masters. This third edition contains all 223 articles from the first 22 volumes of *Share International*.
1st edition 1985. 3rd expanded edition 2004.
ISBN 978-90-71484-29-2, 452pp.

Maitreya's Mission, Volume One

The first of a trilogy of books which describe the emergence and teachings of Maitreya, the World Teacher. As human consciousness steadily matures, many of the ancient 'mysteries' are now being revealed. This volume can be seen as a guidebook for humanity as it travels on the evolutionary journey. The book's canvas is vast: from the new teachings of the Christ to meditation and karma; from life after death, and reincarnation, to healing and social transformation; from initiation and the role of service to the Seven Rays; from Leonardo da Vinci and Mozart to Sathya Sai Baba. It sets the scene and prepares the way for the work of Maitreya, as World Teacher, and the creation of a new and better life for all. It is a powerful message of hope.

1st edition 1986. 3rd edition 1993, reprinted 2003. ISBN 978-90-71484-08-7, 419pp.

Maitreya's Mission, Volume Two

This inspiring and heart-warming book offers new hope and guidance to a suffering world on the threshold of a Golden Age. It presents the teachings of Maitreya, the World Teacher, on both the outer, practical, and inner, spiritual levels; His uniquely accurate forecasts of world events, which have astonished international media; and His miraculous appearances which have brought hope and inspiration to many thousands. It also contains a series of unique interviews with Benjamin Creme's Master which throw new and revealing light on some of the greatest problems facing humanity.

This book covers an enormous range: Maitreya's teachings; the growth of consciousness; new forms of government; commercialization and market forces; the principle of sharing; life in the New Age; schools without walls; the Technology of Light; crop circles; the Self; telepathy; disease and death; energy and thought; Transmission Meditation; the soul's purpose. Also includes transcripts of Benjamin Creme's inspiring talks on 'The Overcoming of Fear' and 'The Call to Service'.

1st edition 1993, reprinted 2004. ISBN 978-90-71484-11-7, 753pp.

The Ageless Wisdom Teaching

An overview of humanity's spiritual legacy, this booklet serves as a concise and easy-to-understand introduction to the Ageless Wisdom Teaching. It explains the basic tenets of esotericism, including: source of the Teaching; the emergence of the World Teacher; rebirth and reincarnation; the Law of Cause and Effect; the Plan of evolution; origin of man; meditation and service; future changes. Also included is an esoteric glossary and a recommended reading list.

1st edition 1996, reprinted 2006. ISBN 978-90-71484-13-1, 76pp

Maitreya's Mission, Volume Three

Benjamin Creme presents a compelling vision of the future. With Maitreya, the World Teacher, and His disciples the Masters of Wisdom openly offering Their guidance, humanity will create a civilization worthy of its divine potential. Peace will be established; sharing the world's resources the norm; maintaining our environment a top priority. The new education will teach the fact of the soul and the evolution of consciousness. The cities of the world will be transformed into centres of great beauty.

This book offers invaluable wisdom on a vast range of topics. It includes Maitreya's priorities for the future, and interviews with a Master of Wisdom on 'The Challenge of the 21st Century'. It explores karma and reincarnation, the origin of humanity, meditation and service, the Plan of evolution, and other fundamental concepts of the Ageless Wisdom Teachings. It includes a fascinating look from an esoteric, spiritual perspective at 10 famous artists – among them Leonardo da Vinci, Michelangelo and Rembrandt – by Benjamin Creme, himself an artist.

Like the first two volumes of Maitreya's Mission, this work combines profound spiritual truths with practical solutions to today's most vexing problems. It is indeed a message of hope for a humanity ready to "begin the creation of a civilization such as this world has never yet seen".

1st edition 1997. ISBN 978-90-71484-15-5, 705pp.

The Great Approach: New Light and Life for Humanity

This prophetic book addresses the problems of our chaotic world and its gradual change under the influence of a group of perfected men, the Masters of Wisdom, Who, with Their leader Maitreya, the World Teacher, are returning openly to the world for the first time in 98,000 years.

The book covers such topics as: sharing; the USA in a quandary; ethnic conflicts; crime and violence; environment and pollution; genetic engineering; science and religion; the nature of light; health and healing; education; miracles; the soul and incarnation. An extraordinary synthesis of knowledge, it throws a searchlight on the future; with clear vision it predicts our highest achievements of thought to reveal the amazing scientific discoveries which lie ahead. It shows us a world in which war is a thing of the past, and the needs of all are met.

1st edition 2001. ISBN 978-90-71484-23-0, 320pp.

The Art of Co-operation

The Art of Co-operation deals with the most pressing problems of our time, and their solution, from the point of view of the Ageless Wisdom Teachings that, for millennia, have revealed the forces underlying the outer world. Benjamin Creme brings these teachings up to date, preparing the way for the imminent emergence of Maitreya, the World Teacher, and His group of Masters of Wisdom.

This volume looks at a world locked in ancient competition, trying to solve its problems by old and out-worn methods, while the answer – co-operation – lies in our own hands. It shows the way to a world of justice, freedom and peace through a growing appreciation of the unity underlying all life. Maitreya will inspire in us this growing realization.

Topics include: the necessity of co-operation; the USA and competition; organism versus organization; opportunity for service; fear of loss; karma; love; courage and detachment;

overcoming of glamour; how the Masters teach; unity in diversity; consensus; trust.

1st edition 2002. ISBN 978-90-71484-26-1, 235pp.

Maitreya's Teachings: The Laws of Life

We do not have even fragments of the teachings of former World Teachers given prior to certain knowledge of Their existence. We do not have the teachings of a Christ, or a Buddha, or a Krishna, except seen through the eyes of later followers. For the first time we are given the flavour of the thoughts and insights of a Being of immeasurable stature to enable us to understand the path of evolution stretching ahead of us which He has come to outline for us. The impression left in the mind by the Teacher is that the breadth and depth of His knowledge and awareness have no limits; that He is tolerant and wise beyond conception, and of amazing humility.

Few could read from these pages without being changed. To some the extraordinary insights into world events will be of major interest, while to others the laying bare of the secrets of self-realization, the simple description of experienced truth, will be a revelation. To anyone seeking to understand the Laws of Life, these subtle and pregnant insights will take them quickly to the core of Life itself, and provide them with a simple path stretching to the mountain-top. The essential unity of all life is underscored in a clear and meaningful way. Never, it would appear, have the Laws by which we live seemed so natural and so unconstraining.

1st edition, 2005. ISBN 978-90-71484-31-5, 258pp.

The Art of Living: Living Within the Laws of Life

Inspired by the writings of two Masters of Wisdom, the Master Djwhal Khul and particularly Benjamin Creme's own Master, Part One of this book considers the experience of living as a form of art, like painting or music. To reach a high level of expression requires both knowledge of and adherence to certain fundamental principles. In the art of life, it is through the understanding of the great Law of Cause and Effect, and the related Law of Rebirth, that we achieve the poised harmlessness that leads to personal happiness, right human relations and the correct path for all humanity on its evolutionary journey.

Parts Two and Three, 'The Pairs of Opposites' and 'Illusion', propose that it is man's unique position in the evolutionary scheme – the meeting point of spirit and matter – that produces his seemingly endless struggle both within himself and in outer living. The means by which he emerges from the fog of illusion, and blends these two aspects of himself into one perfect Whole, is living life itself with growing detachment and objective self-awareness.

1st edition 2006. ISBN 978- 90-71484-37-7, 215pp.

~ ~ ~

The above books are published by Share International Foundation (Amsterdam, London). Most have been translated and published in Dutch, French, German, Japanese and Spanish by groups responding to this message. Some have also been published in Chinese, Croatian, Finnish, Greek, Hebrew, Italian, Portuguese, Romanian, Russian, Slovenian and Swedish. Further translations are planned. Books, as well as audio and video cassettes, are available from local booksellers.

SHARE INTERNATIONAL

A unique magazine featuring each month: up-to-date information about the emergence of Maitreya, the World Teacher; an article from a Master of Wisdom; expansions of the esoteric teachings; Benjamin Creme's answers to a wide variety of topical and esoteric questions; articles by and interviews with people at the forefront of progressive world change; news from UN agencies and reports of positive developments in the transformation of our world.

Share International brings together the two major directions of New Age thinking — the political and the spiritual. It shows the synthesis underlying the political, social, economic and spiritual changes now occurring on a global scale, and seeks to stimulate practical action to rebuild our world along more just and compassionate lines.

Share International covers news, events and comments related to Maitreya's priorities: an adequate supply of the right food, housing and shelter for all, healthcare and education as universal rights, and the maintenance of ecological balance in the world.

ISSN 0169-1341

Versions of *Share International* are available in Dutch, French, German, Japanese, Romanian, Slovenian and Spanish. For subscription information, contact the appropriate office below.

For North, Central and South America,
Australia, New Zealand and the Philippines
Share International
PO Box 971, North Hollywood, CA 91603, USA

For the UK
Share International
PO Box 3677, London NW5 1RU, UK

For the rest of the world
Share International
PO Box 41877, 1009 DB Amsterdam, Holland

Extensive information and excerpts from the magazine are published online at: **www.share-international.org**

ABOUT THE AUTHOR

Scottish-born painter and esotericist Benjamin Creme has for over 30 years been preparing the world for the most extraordinary event in human history — the return of our spiritual mentors to the everyday world.

Benjamin Creme has appeared on television, radio and in documentary films worldwide and lectures throughout Western and Eastern Europe, the USA, Japan, Australia, New Zealand, Canada and Mexico.

Trained and supervised over many years by his own Master, he began his public work in 1974. In 1982 he announced that the Lord Maitreya, the long-awaited World Teacher, was living in London, ready to present Himself openly when invited by the media to do so. This event is now imminent.

Benjamin Creme continues to carry out his task as messenger of this inspiring news. His books, thirteen at present, have been translated into many languages. He is also the editor of *Share International* magazine, which circulates in over 70 countries. He accepts no money for any of this work.

Benjamin Creme lives in London, is married, and has three children.